"WHERE SKY AND LINCOLNSHIRE AND WATER MEET"

"WHERE SKY AND LINCOLNSHIRE AND WATER MEET"

To Carmela
Hope you enjoy!

C. Sampson.

Carole Sampson

authorHOUSE®

AuthorHouse™
1663 Liberty Drive
Bloomington, IN 47403
www.authorhouse.com
Phone: 1-800-839-8640

First published by AuthorHouse   10/27/2011

ISBN: 978-1-4567-8959-6 (sc)
ISBN: 978-1-4567-8960-2 (ebk)

Printed in the United States of America

Any people depicted in stock imagery provided by Thinkstock are models, and such images are being used for illustrative purposes only. Certain stock imagery © Thinkstock.

This book is printed on acid-free paper.

For

David and Jackie

Acknowledgements

My thanks to AuthorHouse for giving me this opportunity to publish, and to Ann Merrin for her editing skills and friendship. My deepest thanks to my wonderful husband, David, for his knowledge, advice, support, encouragement and belief in me. Carole is delighted with the work of the illustrator, Susan Shorter, as it catches the flavour of the book.

Chapter 1   Life at 'The Big House'

Amy burst into tears and flung herself on to the bed. She had made such a mess of her life. Handing a baby over to a Welfare Officer was something that she had never envisaged.

How could she have thought that her life would be unaffected by the events of 1944? Why had she not realized that her husband would react in this way?

She felt that her heart would break.

How would this predicament affect her precious first born? Would she miss her new sister? It need not have been like this, if only . . .

Why did it have to be *him* that had returned safely?
Why was she being made to feel guilty, humiliated, dirty?

He had taken their small daughter out, away from the house of shame and heartache.

Would they come back? Would she lose both her babies on the same day?

Perhaps her mother, Alice, always an anchor and support whatever the storm, could have helped if she had been around. Alice always had an answer for a problem even when she was unwell. *He* had insisted that *he* was now all that was necessary to keep the household in order. Her parents were no longer needed.

Amy knew that her mother would not have landed herself in such a situation.

She recalled Alice's stories of the green fields, which stretched further than the eye could see and the ripe, yellow corn which waved in the breeze, where Alice had grown up. She had told Amy of the peaceful aura in the grounds, although as a young girl she had had no idea that Woolston Hall was in such a beautiful part of the country. She had never ventured further than the town nearby but as she grew older she had started to feel restless. She had only experienced life on the estate and with the onset of adulthood, Alice found it was becoming mundane.

The grounds of the house offered opportunities for walking, which, in turn, allowed Alice the quietness to think about her position.

At one time she had wondered if she should leave Woolston Hall and go further afield and find a job in a House away from the rest of her family. Her eldest sister and brother-in-law had found a position as Housekeeper and Gardener on an estate in the south of the county. This meant that they did not visit very often, but it enabled them to raise their family with little discomfort and they seemed to be very happy.

Woolston Hall was a grand, stately home which had once belonged to a noble family who were kin of Cecil, Lord Burghley, during Elizabeth1's prosperous reign. Portraits hung from splendid cornices, magnificent rooms led off long galleries and old tapestries, presents from the Orient, covered old walls. The kitchen had been updated and was the hub of life, although the lady of the house was often seen organising the menus and helping when guests were due.

Lady Dorothy and Sir Howard Hope had a large personal army to regiment their home. Their Head Groom, Frederick, was an important link in the smooth running of their stables whilst his wife, Louisa, was the assistant cook in the kitchen.

Before coming to the Hall, Frederick Smythe and Louisa, who were Alice's parents, had moved into The Stables in the next village when Alice was a small child. Frederick had been delighted to run his own business, especially as it was with his beloved horses. There was a family myth that Louisa's grandmother had been a Spanish gypsy, whose family had fled across the English Channel in the late 18th century, at the time of the Peninsular War, when troops were led by Wellington and Napoleon. Maybe this was why Louisa shared her husband's love of horses and why three of their children had flaming red hair and flashing green eyes, as well as a stunning sense of rhythm, which were to come out in later generations.

Frederick's business had made him a good living, but as time went on money became an issue for him. Everyone who had wanted horses seemed to have established stables of their own, employed their own grooms and no longer needed the services that The Stables could offer. Frederick and Louisa considered moving away into Leicestershire or even changing their life-style completely.

On one of her few visits, Louisa's sister, Olive, who worked as a chamber-maid at Woolston Hall, reported that The Hopes were in need of an assistant cook. Louisa felt that this was a position she could fill. Her family, especially Frederick, often complimented her on her cooking. The Smythes decided that this was the way forward, so the following day Louisa put on her best attire and Frederick prepared the pony and trap for the short journey to Woolston Hall.

Louisa presented herself at the servants' door and her sister introduced her to Mrs. Hill, the Housekeeper, who asked her pertinent questions about her cooking ability. Once Mrs. Hill was satisfied, she asked Louisa to wait in the kitchen whilst she consulted with Lady Dorothy Hope. Louisa was summoned to Lady Dorothy's sitting room, which was simply but cosily furnished with blue as the dominant colour. Lady Dorothy was seated in a winged velvet chair and told Louisa that Mrs. Hill had spoken highly of her.

"If you are as reliable as your sister, Olive, I shall be delighted to have you in my employment", she said.

It was arranged that she should start after the weekend. Frederick was delighted to hear the news and on the way back to The Stables he told her about his conversation with one of the grooms.

"They say that the Head Groom is getting too old and will be leaving his job soon. The Hopes have arranged to keep him in the West Wing, but relieve him of his duties."

"Does this mean that Lord Hope will need a Head Groom?" asked Louisa.

"Um." replied Frederick smugly.

"If only . . . that would be the answer to all our prayers."

Alice had been eight when her parents moved their family into the tied cottage on The Woolston Estate. The cottage had its own small garden in which the Smythes grew vegetables, hollyhocks, roses, gilliflowers, peonies, tulips, marigolds and lilies, courtesy of the gardener at The Hall, who had become a close friend of the family.

When the servants had a free evening, they often met in each other's homes for a chat and a sing-a-long, or had a walk together in the grounds if the weather was good.

Alice had a wonderful childhood and with her siblings spent hours in the grounds of the Hall, either exploring or letting their imagination run riot, sending them to foreign lands or into dangerous dungeons.

When she was younger Alice was not allowed to go into the kitchen, but she had heard from her sister, who worked as a kitchen maid alongside her mother, that it was a very happy place. When Alice became fourteen, she too was employed as a kitchen maid.

Sometimes, Cook allowed her to place the pan of vegetables on the range after she had peeled and sliced them. Despite the nature of her simple tasks, she had nothing to complain about, as everyone was very kind to her and she was thankful for those blessings. Alice wondered if it was her relationship to the much feted Head Groom that made others treat her with such kindness, rather than because of her own virtues.

After years of her contented lifestyle, Alice felt guilty about the restlessness that was beginning to surface in her soul. Her older sister said it was because there were so many changes and the general atmosphere had altered since the turn of the century. There were, however, 'new beginnings' on the horizon.

Most of Alice's older sisters and brothers had long fled the nest and the sister who was still at home with her was expecting a child. The expected addition to the family had been fathered by the stable boy, so Bella would be living at home with their mother and father until old enough to marry her sweetheart, if they still felt that this was what they wanted when the time came.

Alice frequently wondered what it was like to be in love with someone. She had not experienced the tingles and churnings that her sister related to her—until Vincent was appointed as Groom to work in the stables.

He was the eldest boy, the second child of eight children born to William, a cattle dealer, and Eliza Rogers, who lived near Nottingham.

He came to the kitchen for breakfast and lunch in between grooming and exercising the horses, so Alice came into regular contact with him. He was taller than Alice. Handsome, with dark hair. His outside life gave him the swarthy look that sat so well on young men.

The Summer Ball at Woolston Hall was imminent and Vincent asked Alice to accompany him. It was a huge thrill for her and the event led to further walkings out, an engagement and marriage.

Once she was married, living in another tied cottage, Alice took on a radiance and beauty that was often remarked on by the family. She and Vincent produced four children, including a dainty girl who had been named Amy, after her great-grandmother.

Amy was pretty, with a heart-shaped face and slightly auburn hair which hung in ringlets round her face and shoulders. She was of a gentle disposition. She spoke with her eyes and her ready smile always engaged people in conversation. Adults were anxious that these attributes would lead to trouble for Amy and often chastened her mother for not disciplining her more radically than she did, but Alice only smiled graciously at these comments. She often thought about them when she was alone, but had no idea how she should respond to Amy's ways, so left things to take their own course.

Childhood was exciting for Amy and her siblings. They were able to play in the garden of their tied cottage or venture further afield on The Estate. Amy became an accomplished needle-woman, like her mother and grandmother, and made many small garments for the dolls in the cottage. She also enjoyed physical activities and could climb a tree as quickly as her brothers. Her love of horses came from spending hours at the stables with her father and she wished that she could ride at the side of The Hopes' sons and daughters; but she realised from a young age that she was not of the upper class and that some dreams had to remain so.

Amy liked clothes and pretty trinkets, which were difficult to obtain as England was at war with Germany during the first six years of her life. The Hopes lost two sons in The Great War and many of their employees were affected by loss. Alice's two elder brothers were killed at the battle of The Somme and Frederick also lost a brother and a cousin in the same carnage. There was sadness in The Hall, but Lord and Lady Hope tried to ensure that their servants did not suffer in any way. They were good employers, who truly cared for the people whom they had sheltered through a difficult time.

When Amy was 14, she joined her mother in the kitchen and learned how to cook—this would ensure she would make someone a good wife.

Amy started to keep a diary and enjoyed entering her thoughts and little anecdotes. Entries often mentioned the weather or the personnel at the House or the monotonous days of living. Occasionally she mentioned a film she had seen with her sister or mother at the cinema in Sleaford. Greta Garbo was her favourite star and she dreamed about the situations she saw on film and wondered if her life would be as vivid as Greta's life was.

She was certain that her future was not going to be where her present life lay.

Sometimes Alice and Vincent discussed Amy's prospects. Amy rarely ventured further than the nearby village hall dances which were held each month and everyone expected her to marry one of the stable lads or the labourers on the farm. On occasion she accompanied her parents to the nearby town when they needed to attend to important business either for themselves or for their employers.

Chapter 2   Falling For A Uniform

Lincolnshire is a large rural county, 90miles from north to south and 50miles from east to west. Large flat areas with acres of Fenland make it a very beautiful county. An arterial road runs through the county, and the terrain and position make it an ideal site for airfields.

RAF Cranwell was only a few miles away.

Cranwell had been the Admiralty Airfield in World War 1, training naval pilots, before becoming the RAF Cadet College and School of Technical Training. The Electrical and Wireless School was moved from RAF Flowerdown in 1929 and it was renamed RAF College. It was a huge complex, covering acres of land and was a very imposing place.

Amy had seen the fine young men in uniform when she had visited Sleaford. The thrill of the prospect of being married to a handsome man in the RAF filled her thoughts as she laboured over the kitchen range.

One day during the coffee break, Toby, the stable lad, who had a soft spot for Amy asked,

"Have you seen the posters in the village?"

"No," answered Amy. "What are they for?"

"There's going to be a dance at Sleaford Assembly Rooms in aid of some charity."

"When's that then?"

"Oh, next month, I think it said," replied the stable lad.

"That sounds good," enthused Mabel, Amy's friend, colleague and confidante. "We'll have to find out about it, won't we Amy?"

"Oh yes," replied Amy, with a smile.

When Toby had returned to the stables and Amy was alone with Mabel, she mischievously asked,

"Do you think any of the RAF blokes will be there?"

"Let's hope so," giggled Mabel in reply. "When we go for a walk on Sunday afternoon we'll have a look at Toby's poster and then we can make plans!"

On their walk, they scrutinised the poster that Toby had told them about and discovered that 'the dance' was at 7pm on the 8th June 1932. There was no indication that there would be RAF personnel present, but as Mabel said,

"It doesn't say the RAF blokes WON'T be there."

Throughout the month, the forthcoming dance was the topic of conversation with the two friends.

Would their dreams be fulfilled at the dance at Sleaford Assembly Rooms?

Would they find that RAF blokes were their 'type'?

Should they be content to marry stable lads and settle down in tied cottages as their parents had years before them?

"I just feel that I am going to meet the man of my dreams," confided Amy to her friend.

"What will he look like then?"

"Oh! Tall, dark and handsome . . . it would be nice if he looked like one of the film stars—like Lewis Stone."

"Like in 'Wild Orchids' that we saw the other month," said Mabel.

"Umm," replied Amy with eyes that shone like stars.

"Well at least you can dream!"

Mabel felt that Amy tended to live in a fantasy world, but perhaps there was little harm in having these thoughts. She, herself, would rather fall for someone she knew and who her parents rated; marriage was a big step and Mabel wanted security.

Before the girls could attend a dance, there were chores to be done in order to prepare for the big occasion, so Amy learned a few of her mother's tricks in creativity and thrift!

The girls practised the dances that they had learned as children so that they could waltz and dance a reasonable quickstep, taking turns to 'be the man' so that there would be no confusion on their big night out. Amy responded easily to music and learned steps and turns with little effort. She felt that she had been created to dance.

Her excitement was tangible.

Eventually the 8th June arrived. Amy and Mabel were dressed in long gowns, which Alice had made for them from unused dress lengths of material that she had been given by Lady Hope at The Hall.

Alice and Vincent walked the girls to the bus stop, which would take them into Sleaford.

"Do you think we'll meet the man of our dreams, Mr. Rogers?" asked Mabel.

"Don't be too hasty, Mabel. There's plenty of time for that."

"You aren't often lucky at your first dance," smiled Amy's mother.

Mr. Rogers turned to the two young girls.

"You both look grand," he said. "Enough to make a saint turn to women. So you make sure you behave yourselves and I'll be waiting for you both at half past eleven outside the Assembly Rooms. O.K.?"

The girls nodded excitedly and Alice kissed them affectionately as they went off to Sleaford on the bus in the early evening.

When they reached the Assembly Rooms, the two girls walked up the steps and made an elegant entrance into the huge Dance Hall where the band was already playing a popular waltz.

Amy was instantly captivated by the decorations, the lights, the atmosphere and the band.

"Isn't it beautiful," she gasped.

"I love this music," replied Mabel, looking round the room. "AND there are RAF blokes here!"

"It's SO exciting. I do hope Mr. Right is here. I'm fed up with stable lads and the smell of horses."

"Come off it, Amy. The lads are jolly nice—and we know where we are with them."

"What do you mean?"

"Well, these men could be anyone. We don't know their families or the towns they're from—they could be ANYONE."

"Don't be a spoil sport, Mabel. Let's enjoy ourselves and see . . . Look, there are some blokes looking at us."

It wasn't long before the young RAF men had noticed the pretty girls and Amy found herself in William's arms. His charm, his looks and his uniform were all proof to Amy that this could be her future husband, so when he asked if he could meet her on Sunday afternoon, she readily agreed.

The dance came to an end all too quickly for Amy, but her father was waiting in the pony and trap. On the way home to Woolston Hall, she chattered excitedly about the dance and her partner whilst her father patted her arm knowingly. They dropped Mabel at her cottage where she ran into her mother's arms.

"You'll be making a wedding dress yet, Mother," Vincent announced to his wife when they arrived home. "Our Amy's well smitten with her RAF chappie."

Alice looked at her daughter's radiant face.

"Now don't get too excited, Amy, he may have other fish to fry that you don't know about."

"Oh, I'm sure he hasn't mother. He didn't talk about anyone."

"Did he tell you anything about his family?" asked Alice.

"Well not really. We danced a lot and it was too noisy to talk much. I do know that his father was a Major in the Army, so he should be a good catch, if that's what you mean," retorted Amy.

"Now then, my girl, enough of that. Your mother is only concerned for you."

Amy smiled at her mother, begging her to understand how she was feeling inside.

"Is there another date on the carpet then?" continued Amy's father, knowing that this could be the start of more worry for him.

"I think there is another dance before Christmas which we said we'd meet at," answered Amy.

"O.K. We'll have to see what the notices say when we next go into Sleaford," smiled Mr. Rogers. "Meanwhile, it's time we all made our way up wooden hill or we shan't be fit for the morning. Goodnight my little one. Sweet dreams," he said, kissing his last born on the forehead.

"But, . . . he has asked to see me next Sunday on my day off."

"Well, that should be alright," smiled Mr. Rogers. "Is he coming over here so I can meet him?"

"Yes. I thought you'd prefer that. He'll be here about 2 o'clock, after lunch."

"That's good. I'd like to see who's captured my little girl's heart so quickly," said Mrs. Rogers. "Now off you go. It's getting late . . . Sleep well."

"Night, Father, Mother," said Amy, dropping a fond kiss on her mother's cheek. "Thank you for taking such good care of me. It helped to make tonight extra special," she added, twirling round in her dance dress.

Amy skipped across the room and opened the door to the stairs.

"She's too excited to sleep," laughed Mr. Rogers.

"At least we'll meet him very soon. I'll feel better then," said Amy's mother. "We'll have a cup of tea and then wend our way up, eh?"

Amy felt elated. She had never danced so much in her life and the thrill she felt was beyond her expectations. She had enjoyed being held and swung round by William and began to wonder if this was what her sister had meant when she talked about love.

She had been warned about daydreaming and having a romanticised idea of love, but she had never experienced these feelings in her life.

Before she settled to sleep, she opened her diary and wrote up her entry for this special day.

Excerpts from Amy's diary:

8th June 1932
Met a super young chap tonight at the dance. He's tall and handsome and treated me like gold dust. We danced nearly every dance. His name is William and he is in the Air Force at RAF Cranwell; he's a turner—whatever that is! His father was a Major in the Army. He says he wants to meet up on Sunday. He's coming to the cottage—thought M and F would like that. Can't wait. Looking forward to the next dance in Sleaford. Mabel enjoyed herself with a lad from east Lancs, but isn't expecting anything to come of it.

16th. June 1932
Meeting with parents went well. Mother said she thought him very well mannered and refined. Father said that was because he is from service stock and his father being an officer will know how to behave. Mother said that it was a good job we had all lived at The Hall so we knew all about refinement.
After the meet we went for a walk round The Estate.
William held my hand and we told each other about our families—mother was pleased! He left at 5.30. Seeing him in a fortnight. Have I met the man of my dreams?.

Amy's days were interspersed with thoughts of William. She sparkled.
Toby asked her out, but she told him that she was already taken, but wanted to stay as his friend.

"Plenty of other fish in the sea," he laughed, but he was very sad that he hadn't captured her heart, as she had his.

Mabel became interested in Toby and she confessed to Amy that she had always liked him. She had been reticent to show her feelings because she knew he liked her friend. Now that Amy was involved with William, Mabel felt that she could let her feelings for Toby show more openly.

It seemed that life was becoming more settled at The Hall. William visited as often as his duties allowed and was introduced to Amy's sisters and brothers. He seemed to be at ease with everyone including the children.

The four friends went to the dance at Sleaford Assembly Rooms in November and it was as magical for Amy as the first dance. Toby and Mabel decided that they would marry as soon as Mabel was twenty-one, so it was an exciting time.

Amy wished that she had a wedding to look forward to, but as Mrs. Rogers said,

"Mabel and Toby have known each other for a very long time. The families know each other and she will get instant support when she needs it."

That was meant to make Amy feel better. Although she was pleased for her friend, she longed for her own married life to begin.

Woolston Hall announced its usual Christmas Dance and there was much preparation in the kitchen. It was customary for Lord & Lady Hope to entertain guests for dinner before the dance. Lady Dorothy had purchased Mrs. Beeton's book on 'Household Management', which she was very keen on using, so Cook referred to it for the big occasion.

She felt sure that she could provide the set menu from 'A dinner for twelve people', even though there would be forty guests. After some discussion with the more mathematically inclined Housekeeper and Butler, it was decided that she could quadruple the amounts in the recipe. She put forward this idea to Lady Dorothy, explaining to her mistress that the Housekeeper had suggested that the servants could enjoy the leftovers! Lady Hope agreed.

The kitchen buzzed with activity as 'soup a la Reine' and 'Julienne soup' were prepared. Turbot and lobster sauce and slices of salmon a la Genevese to follow and, as Mrs. Beeton had suggested, croquettes of leveret, fricandeau of veal, and vol au vent with stewed mushrooms should be served as entrees. Guinea fowls and forequarter of lamb were the next dishes to be prepared and, after charlotte a la Parisienne, lobster salad with kale, orange jelly, meringues, ratafia ice pudding and, dessert and ices were to be served.

"They'll never be able to dance after that lot," exclaimed Amy.

"Well you youngsters will be able to enjoy yourselves on the dance floor all the more!" laughed Cook.

As Lord and Lady Hope had included her staff in the guests to attend the dance, Amy's mother had once again put her dressmaking skills to work. Amy, Mabel and Alice looked as radiant as everyone else did for the grand occasion.

William had been included in the family invitation and as Toby was an employee of The Hall, the friends were certain of enjoying the Christmas Dance.

December 1932
What a super time. Christmas dances have always been fun at the Hall, but this was something special. Ma and Pa are thrilled with William and Ma commented on the fact that he was so attentive!! Think I'm in love . . .

During the winter months, Amy and William enjoyed walks in the grounds of the estate; tea with Amy's parents; visiting the cinema in Sleaford to watch her beloved Greta Garbo and Lewis Stone. There was news of a new find in Cary Grant and they were looking forward to seeing him when the film arrived in Sleaford. Amy's father had told her that Cary Grant's real name was Archibald Leach and that he had been born in Bristol in the South West of England. Grant had gone off to the States when he was a young boy with a circus and had found his way to the theatre and then to Hollywood. William said that he could understand why he had succeeded because Cary Grant was a fine looking man. If he was any good in films, he'd have women falling over him.

Amy was longing to meet William's mother, but there always seemed to be a reason why a visit could not be arranged. His father, who had been an Army Officer, was dead and Amy decided that Mrs. Jackson must have fallen on hard times.

Eventually, William announced that he would like to take Amy to meet his mother. It meant a train journey to Grantham, but that was exciting for Amy who had never experienced one before.

Alice ensured that Amy had a pretty dress and matching coat, hat and gloves by using her extraordinary skills with the needle, and steam from the kettle which reshaped an old hat she had worn at one of the weddings in the family. In fact, it had had many an outing in different guises and no one appeared to notice that it was the same hat revamped.

Amy was very excited when her father took her to meet William at the station. They intended to return that evening and William was going to stay over with the Rogers, as he had a few days leave. On the train, William explained that his mother had not recovered from the death of her husband or losing her home on the Army base and she was eventually admitted to a Home for the Elderly in Grantham, which was near his sister.

"Will she know you, William?" asked Amy.

"Oh yes. And she'll know you!" he laughed.

"How?" Amy asked innocently.

"Because I've told her about you."

"Oh. How lovely."

William explained that the Home was reasonably well run and that the Army helped with the fees, so he and his sister were content with the set up.

The meeting between Amy and Mrs. Jackson went well and both of the women appeared to like each other, which pleased William.

Amy discovered that William usually spent his leave with his sister and her family, visiting his mother each day when he was around.

She realised that she had been completely wrapped up in her new-found life and her own family that she had not pressed William on details of his family, so she vowed to ask him lots of questions about 'life before Amy' whilst he was on leave with them.

He had not enjoyed his childhood in the same way as she had and was pleased to join the RAF as soon as he could. He was not extravert in nature and had found it difficult to make friends, particularly with members of the opposite sex. Since Reginald had joined the unit, William had been happier, because he was out-going and had encouraged him to join clubs and learn to dance, which was why they had started going to the dances in Sleaford. Another mate, Bob, had an old car, which they clambered into when they explored towns together. But, generally, William was a quiet person who enjoyed his own company (as much as is possible in a hut that was shared with nine other men) and he intended to better himself in his career with the RAF.

Amy's family liked William, so everyone waited with bated breath to see if Amy was to be the next daughter to be married.

June 1933
Bill asked me to marry him. SO excited. Father says he'll be proud to have him as a son-in-law. Mother asked if I'm sure that I want to become Mrs. Jackson . . . can't wait!!
Will have to wait till next year when I'm 21. What a stupid law . . . Mother says I mustn't let us get carried away as she doesn't want to be a grandmother yet. Must be careful.

August 1933
It is SO wonderful to be in love. I have a lovely ring-sapphires and diamonds that Bill got from jewelers in Sleaford. We shall have to wait for somewhere to live. Have no intention of living with ma and pa. Anyway, Bill will have to be near the base.
His mates have told him he is lucky to have found such a nice family to join . . .

William put in the application for married quarters at the Base and as soon as he heard that he could have a house in August 1934, he told Amy's parents so that their wedding could be organised. The wedding was to be at the village church and Mabel was to be Amy's bridesmaid whilst her two married sisters would be matrons of honour.

Alice had wondered if the nieces should attend their aunt, but her daughters had wanted the privilege.

December 1933
We have set the date for August 4th. Can't wait. Mabel has agreed to be a bridesmaid, along with Beth and Olive. Ma says she'll see if Mrs. Hope can give her some old material to make up into dresses. Pa has offered to ask for the use of a carriage and four to take us to church! It'll be magical.

There was the usual Christmas Ball at Woolston Hall and the kitchens were very busy for a few weeks. Relatives of The Hopes came to stay, so the servants did not have a spare moment with the demands of the hosts and their guests.

William was unable to attend the Ball, as his sister demanded that he return to Grantham and the family on the two days of leave that he was allowed. He and Amy were able to spend the New Year together at the cottage. Beth and her family joined them and as she was able to play the piano, there was much singing of Christmas Carols.

January 1934
We were able to be together for New Year. To think, next New Year we shall be an old married couple. Perhaps family will be coming to our house for celebrations! It was lovely to be able to sing the Christmas carols as a family.

February 1934
Lady Dorothy has offered us the small hall for the wedding reception and has told mother that the kitchen will supply the wedding feast—their present! Mother and father are amazed at their generosity and I have to write a note to thank their—ships(!) for being so kind to us. At least The Hopes are pleasant in comparison to some employers—some of the stories that my sisters tell about the families they work for are really frightening.

Life for The Rogers continued in its usual mundane way. Amy's excitement sometimes made her mother fear that her daughter had unrealistic expectations of married life. Alice tried to explain that young love could not sustain its intensity for ever, but despite all her mother's efforts, Amy was not to be moved from a feeling that her dreams had been fulfilled when William came into her life.

July 1934
Shall be married to my Bill soon. Fancy, I shall be Mrs. Jackson . . . sounds good! Mother has told me that I could be disappointed if I continue to think that life will be as blissful as this forever, but I know we'll be alright. She has made me a lovely dress from some old sheets trimmed with lace and the bridesmaids will be in matching frocks made from the blue velvet curtains out of the Hall drawing room. Mrs. Hope said she'd 'be delighted for Mum to use them for the purpose'.

Chapter 3   Early Days

August was a glorious month and the weather held for the wedding. Everyone enjoyed the special day, which went without any hitches and The Hopes enabled their employees to relax from the troubles and demands of in-service life.

William and Amy were able to have a short honeymoon in The Midlands, which incorporated a visit to old Mrs. Jackson in The Home. They stayed at a small Bed and Breakfast in the centre of Grantham and enjoyed each other's company. William told Amy that there were rumours of a new course starting at the base and that he might be involved in it, as he was becoming an experienced member of the team. Amy nodded and knew that if he was happy, she would be.

In October 1934, Mabel and Toby were married in the village church. As they were both employees of The Hopes, they enjoyed a reception at Woolston Hall and settled to a life of bliss in one of the tied cottages on the estate.

Amy and Mabel remained friends, but it was difficult because Mabel had few days off work and those she had she wanted to spend with her husband. Within two years Mabel had become pregnant and had given birth to a beautiful baby boy and two years later she had twin girls. She told Amy that she would have liked four children, but money was tight and they were not sure if they could afford to increase their family further.

For the first years of marriage, life was idyllic and Amy gave and received love. They were given quarters on the base and Amy delighted in creating a home. She made new curtains from old material sent from her old employer, covered a sofa that was being thrown away and polished up an oak table and chairs that her father had liberated from a disused out house. The family had clubbed together and bought them their bedroom furniture as a wedding present, so the house had become very homely. There was a small garden with enough room to have a lawn and a vegetable patch, which she enjoyed working. Amy was content in the knowledge that she had made the right decision to branch out and move away from domestic service.

She was slightly envious of Mabel's role as mother. No baby had appeared for her and William, despite them taking no precaution against pregnancy and having frequent sex, but Amy's mother told her that God had a reason for her not conceiving and she must be patient.

Gradually, however, William became short-tempered with her and Amy felt that he was disappointed that they had not had a child.

Or perhaps it was connected to the fact that RAF Cranwell had become important to the country, as the 1930s heralded mock battle preparations for the air defence of London. People were urged to make preparation for war as no one knew if it would come in months rather than years. Life had to go on as normal, which proved to be quite easy for Amy, being cocooned in the arms of William and his beloved Airforce. Domestic issues were the ones that dominated her thoughts.

September 1938
Today, I let the soup boil over and it made a mess of the cooker. Bill was furious with me and screamed that I should be more careful. Anyone would think he had to clean it. Money doesn't grow on trees, he said . . . he treats me like an idiot. Of course I know he has to earn it. He was cruel about the wasted vegetables the other day—I just can't use them all up. He grows rows of peas and potatoes and cabbages. It's hard to know what to do with them all. I give some to the neighbours, but they have enough of their own really.
I wish I could get pregnant. That may make life easier—at least it would be another mouth to feed his wretched vegetables to . . .
Mother said that young love never lasts.
I didn't really believe her and he seemed so nice before we were married. He was funny about some things that I didn't care for, but I thought he would change!

Some days his temper got the better of him and William would lash out at her. Afterwards he would be mortified

21

and would hold her to him and express deep sorrow for his actions. But, the outbursts soured their relationship and Amy began to long for the early days when her handsome uniformed beau had wooed her.

March 1939
Still no baby. Why can't we make one? Bill gets more awkward by the day. There's talk of war and he says he'll be glad to get away for a bit. I can't do a lot right for him. Was annoyed that I was in May's today when he got home from work. He came home early, but said that I ought to keep myself to myself more and find jobs to do around the house and garden. Even when I try to keep the house clean and do the mending, the painting to freshen things up and all the baking, it never seems to be enough. It seems that it's impossible to please him.

The Jacksons heard the official announcement that Britain was at war on 3rd September 1939. Many people gathered in Churches to hear the wireless broadcast by Chamberlain, but news travels faster on an RAF base! They had been expecting it more than 'the man in the street', so were not as shocked, but it meant many changes for families because the men would be taken away from them. Amy was almost relieved when she heard the news, because she knew that her irascible husband would be more concerned with work and could even be sent abroad to fight for king and country. She wondered if he would appreciate her more if he had a few months away from her.

In 1940, the ladies on the base responded to Lord Beaverbrook's appeal for aluminium utensils that could be turned into aircraft. As their husbands were directly involved with flying the craft, it made the war seem more real. Amy and her neighbour, May, went to see the contributions that had been made. There was a mountain of saucepans, despite only one from each household being donated to 'the cause.'

"Just shows how many people there are on the base," said May.

"Yes. And we hardly know anyone except those in our road," replied Amy.

"You'd think we'd have met more people considering it's war. I'll have to think of something that'll get us together. There must be poor souls who've already lost loved ones."

"Perhaps we should take more notice of things outside our own front door," said Amy, who realised that May was making a poignant comment.

At the beginning of the war, RAF Cranwell became the RAF College Service Flying Training School and also housed the RAF Hospital. It became the forefront of training: No.1 Electrical & Wireless School; the School of Clerk accounting; Specialist Signals Course; Supplies Depot Course; No.2 Flying Instructors Course and No.3 (coastal) Operational Training Unit.

Once RAF Cranwell was named as the No.1 Electrical and Wireless School, William was kept very busy. He was often tired and introverted, except when something annoyed him within the home, which usually involved a misdemeanour (in his eyes) made by his long-suffering wife.

Initially, war only touched them both through rumour and the wireless. People began to believe that England would never be really at war whilst Chamberlain was Prime Minister, but when a British force was outwitted by the German defeat of Norway, the desire for a new man at the top was felt and Winston Churchill became the leader.

The flight in Britain of a jet powered aircraft in 1941 caused much excitement. When the Gloster E28/39, which was powered by the Whittle jet engine, took off from S Airfield, the event was heralded widely, especially by Cranwell, because Frank Whittle had developed the idea whilst a Flight Cadet in the 1920s.

Within a year many lives had been lost in the Blitz and cinemas and newspapers were awash with pictures and comments. The devastation of towns like Hull and London ensured that people knew Hitler had not finished with Britain. Anderson shelters were made into little homes and many neighbours found camaraderie in sheltering together in these, or in cellars, or under special tables in their homes. No one was safe.

One lady had brought her baby home from the maternity hospital the previous night. Her husband had gone to do his night work at the local factory when there was a raid on her town. She decided she should get to her Anderson shelter, when she heard a bomb drop at the end of her road. As she sheltered her little boy in her arms, she came out of the bedroom and tried to go down the stairs. It was only then that she realised the stairs were no longer there. She made the decision to stay in the bedroom and was rescued by her frantic husband when he arrived home.

By 1942, there was a population of 7,000 at RAF Cranwell and men were being prepared for warfare to take the place of those who had already given their lives for their country. Amy and William spent Christmas 1942 knowing that William was to train in preparation for combat. He was proud that he would be fighting for his country in India, but Amy, along with other wives, wept as the men flew off to their fate, not knowing if they would ever meet again.

It was January 18th.

Amy felt so nauseous that she took herself back to bed once the farewells were completed. She wondered if Bill's departure had been more upsetting than she had at first realised but as the days went by, she knew that she was, at last, pregnant.

February 1943
At last . . . a baby is on the way. It WOULD be just as Bill is going to war. Wonder what he'll think. Still, it'll be lovely to have a tiny being in the house. I expect ma and pa will be over the moon. They, like me, wondered if it would ever happen. Can't wait to buy some wool and a pattern to make some tiny clothes for it—always been doing it for other people up to now. Have told May and she seems as pleased as me. She says I've had a long face every month for years now and will be glad when I can be really happy about being pregnant. Morning sickness is not a nice thing. God must be a man. This war seems to be going on and on, but at least Bill isn't here to moan about me being off colour. I can go and have a rest

whenever I feel like it without being anxious that he'll arrive home and the tea won't be ready. God moves etc.

William was due to go out to India at the end of March, so Amy wrote to him with the news. His reply was ambiguous; he could not be with her, he might be killed, the future was uncertain, but he suggested she kept smiling and enjoy her pregnancy with the support of family and friends.

In 1943, RAF Folkingham near Aslackby, Lincolnshire (which is about ten miles from RAF Cranwell) was converted to a bomber station and transferred to USAAF. It was opened as a USAAF 1X Troop Carrier Command Station flying squadrons of C-47s.

An American command station brought its own excitement to East Anglia in the form of young, less formal, glamorous, generous men who lived for the moment, in case they died in the next raid or drop into enemy land.

Although there were few raids in the area, Amy felt that everyone needed to be cushioned from the horrors of war. Many women that Amy knew had been involved with the loss of a loved one. Her uncle, her mother's youngest brother, had been lost when The Hood went down and her cousin had died at Dunkirk, so she had experienced grief within her own family.

Newsreels at the cinema and billboards outside the shops informed people of the progress in the war. Many women became involved through the Land Army, Civil Defense, aircraft manufacture, the munitions factories, NAAFI (which was the civilian institute which catered for the armed forces) nursing, the Royal Observer Corps, radio industry, tank manufacture and the transport industry.

Pregnancy allowed Amy an exemption, which was a relief to her as she felt that she had few talents to offer a work force, having been in service all her working life. However, she knew that she must do something for the 'war effort'.

The base had its own shop. At May's suggestion, Amy formed a knitting circle, which could produce necessary clothing for children and adults to buy in the shop. There were young women who, like Amy, were exempt and others who were older, who were not conscripted, so a group of twenty women met twice a week to knit cardigans, jumpers, socks and vests for merchandise. They also knitted additional vests and socks which could be sent abroad to troops. Amy enjoyed knitting socks for soldiers, in the belief that William would surely be given the pairs that she had knitted!

She and May also continued to cultivate their gardens to produce vegetables (carrots, cabbage, brussel sprouts and potatoes) as well as the occasional flower, which all could be sold in the shop on the base, as well as keeping themselves and the neighbourhood in healthy, cheap food.

May became a ticket collector at the railway station in Sleaford. She and other women were often at work away from the base, so Amy found herself in demand as a baby-minder after school had finished. She loved being with the children and felt that her exposure to their tantrums, mood swings and fun was a good learning opportunity for her.

April 1943

Children play in a group of four
On the grass outside the door.
All is well at first it seems,
But silence's shattered by the screams—
Breaking silence of the day—cause she can't get her own way!
It'll be like that when I'm a mother
But I'll be pleased to have that bother.
A few more months; it will soon pass by
Then there'll be sleepless nights for me to enjoy.

Not bad for a first attempt since school! The children are so lovely to have here. The weather is exceptional for the time of year, which is a blessing as they can be outside until it gets dusk.
A line from Bill today, but no mention of where he is. May's letter was censored in places; she thinks Stanley must have given too many details. Oh well!
The vegetables are doing well and the knitting circle grows every week, so am doing my bit. It's nice to see everyone. Joan has heard that her brother has been killed and Jane's brother is being

brought home with 'horrific injuries' so they say. I wonder what
that means. Will he be able to walk or hear?
Such sadness. I wonder how Bill really is . . . he never says.

**Loneliness was prevalent during the war. As a remedy people
were encouraged to become more sociable and adopt the
maxim that they 'were all in it together'. Dancing was the
most popular antidote to loneliness, with 'swing' dominating
the sound within the dancehalls. The Americans brought
the 'Lindyhop' (a precursor to the jive) with them, although
dances like 'The Lambeth Walk' gave the gatherings a party
atmosphere. Love ballads dominated the radio and the BBC
was playing Vera Lynn's records more frequently than those
of America's singers.**

**RAF Cranwell was not excluded from these joys of wartime
Britain and Amy was soon to find herself embroiled in the
relief from the tasks that accompanied Chuchill's promise of
'blood, toil, sweat and tears'.**

Chapter 4   Life Without William

As the days lengthened in May, some wives began to take walks around the base and to go into Sleaford on the bus together, but travel became more difficult because the area was busy with war-related events.

Although the knitting circle and the garden kept her busy during the daytime, Amy became bored with cleaning her small house and cooking for herself in the evenings. She found little solace in writing in her diary each day, so she jumped at the opportunity of going to the dance (a monthly event) on the base when her neighbour suggested it to her. The dances were seen as a tonic for the lonely wives and allowed them a few hours to relax away from the horrors of bad news which seemed to strike the base each day.

The American Airmen from the nearby base often attended the dances and arrived laden with gifts, which often included groceries, nylons and make-up. Their easy charm and manner swept many a girl off her feet.

Amy's pregnancy made her radiant and her ready smile and flashing green eyes made an impression on the young men. Dancing was one of Amy's passions and she had a natural talent for all the new crazes, so she enjoyed her monthly jaunts, until she became too cumbersome for swirling around a dance floor.

One night she found herself dancing with a young, fair-haired American who told her his name was Guy. He had a pleasant manner and whirled her round the dance floor with ease. He taught her how to do the Lindyhop, which she picked up easily. They had a good evening, which ended with a cheek-to cheek dance, as was customary in America.

Amy was amazed that someone should hold her so closely to him after only a few dances, but, as she looked around her, it appeared to be the norm in the dance hall. When the evening was over she thought little more of it and concentrated on her pregnancy.

Excerpts from Guy's diary.

May 1943

These dances are more like it. Met a pretty girl who was full of life and a superb dancer. 'An English Rose' as they say. But she wears a wedding ring.

June 1943

Another dance: good. Amy dances like a dream and is a joy to be with. She is obviously pregnant though. Her husband's in India and she says she's looking forward to being a mother. Trust me to fall for a married woman. She's something else!

July 1943

No dance this month so not able to see my English Rose—more the pity. She is even more lovely than the girls back home. Angie stopped writing in the third month of my tour, so expect she's found someone else. What a good job we are stationed so near to Cranwell and that the dances are arranged for us. I'll have to pray that I don't get sent away and that Amy's old man doesn't come back!!!

August 1943

Amy not at the dance tonight, but sent her regards. (I'd have preferred love . . .)The second month that I've not seen her. May says she's too near her time and doesn't want to risk anything. Didn't find anyone else to take Amy's place, although some of the girls can dance pretty well.
The dance wasn't quite the same without her.

Norma Ann was born in September. Amy's mother, Alice, came to the base to be at her side when her time came. The labour was short and with the help of the nurse from the hospital base, she was able to give birth in the front bedroom of her house. Amy felt that she would burst with happiness—a longed-for baby at last!

The women on the base were very supportive of each other and Amy's neighbours rallied round to help her as much as possible, especially in the early months after her mother had returned to the Hall.

A photograph of a proud Amy in the garden holding Norma in her arms was taken by her neighbour and duly dispatched to William in India so that he could see his baby daughter in spite of being miles away from his family. Amy hoped he would comment.

Excerpts from Guy's diary

October 1943
May says Amy had a little girl. I sent my best. Might call on her if I can find out where she hangs out.
Wish I could stop thinking of her. Finding I can't concentrate on my job half the time. The guys tease me about Amy; didn't realise it was so obvious I fancied her.

At first the new baby kept Amy fully occupied and she found true happiness in her role as a mother. She enjoyed changing nappies, washing baby clothes, cooking delicacies, pushing a pram, taking short walks around the roads on the base and chatting with the other women at the knitting circle.

When Norma had her sleep, Amy caught up with the garden weeds if the weather was clement, listened to the radio or wrote letters to her mother and her Bill. It was difficult to communicate with the latter as she rarely heard from him and he was limited in what he was allowed to write to her, so apart from news about Norma, she found herself 'tongue tied' when she tried to put pen to paper.

Her neighbour May tried to help out as much as possible and the girls who were young mothers met weekly at each other's houses to talk and swap baby stories. Norma was a good sleeper and gave her mother little trouble in comparison to what she heard from her contemporaries. Amy felt very blessed.

As no one talked much about missing a husband, Amy rarely mentioned Bill. Although there was a war being fought it took second place to her role of mother.

There were still dances at the base. Amy was too wrapped up in motherhood to consider taking a night off or having time with her friends rather than with Norma. She looked forward to visits from her mother and father which were rare because of their duties.

Guy's diary

November 1943
Amy didn't come to the dance again. Asked May for her address! Sent her some nylons via May.
Have decided I'll drop by and persuade her to come and enjoy herself. Who knows what might happen? Have to keep busy or my fancies take over.

Wives on the base had been warned that their menfolk would not be able to write often. Sometimes, two or three letters arrived together, but William seemed pleased that they had eventually had a child, although he had asked her in one of his letters if she was sure the baby was his. He felt that they had been trying for so long and nothing had happened, but as soon as he went away, Amy had become pregnant. Amy was indignant at this suggestion and confided in May about his bad-tempered outbursts.

Excerpt from Amy's diary

November 1943
Haven't needed to do this for a bit. Motherhood has kept me well occupied. Something will turn up, as ma used to say . . . May says that perhaps Bill is anxious about us. He doesn't like being away from his child that he'd longed for. She also said that we've no idea what is happening to our men as they aren't allowed to even tell us where they are, so I have to be more tolerant. I've not really thought too much about what the men are experiencing. Have been too tied up with my little Norma. Oh GOD please guide me.

It was almost Christmas, the weather was bright but chilly, Amy was rocking Norma to sleep in her pram in the back garden when she heard a knock at the door. She opened it to find the American Airman with whom she often danced at the Base dances.

"Hello," he smiled. "How are you?"

"Oh, fine, thanks. What can I do for you?"

"May I come in?"

"Oh. Yes, of course."

"I've thought about you a lot," he said.

"Oh," replied Amy, who had rarely given him a thought since baby Norma had arrived.

"Did May give you the nylons?"

"Oh yes. Thank you. Very kind."

She suddenly felt shy and awkward. What did this young man want from her? Surely, no one would send such a gift without there being a catch. She was flustered. Where was this leading? She knew of girls who had become involved with Americans and had heard stories of how life had changed by knowing them. They were attentive, charming, confident and exciting to be with.

He was attractive, but Amy had responsibilities now that she was a mother. She should be careful.

"Are you going to come to the dances again?" Guy asked.

"It's difficult now that I'm a mother," she replied.

"I'm sure there must be some way. I heard that a group of girls baby-sit for each other when necessary. You can't let yourself become isolated. Not in this climate. Who knows what might happen tomorrow."

"I'll think about it."

"Don't think."

Norma was obviously aware that something was amiss and let out a huge yell.

"I must get back to the baby," said Amy, ushering out her unexpected guest.

"Hope to see you," he shouted as he roared away in his jeep.

Chapter 5　　　　A Social Life Again

Excerpt from Amy's diary

December 1943
Guy has turned up. He heard that I'd had Norma and wants me to
go back to dancing.
He argues that we should live for the day . . . Can't see Bill
agreeing with that. I'll put Norma first . . . But, it would be nice to
go dancing again. will have to see.
I could wear the nylons. Would save me from drawing a seam up
my leg.

The war became more intense and Amy took solace in her
occasional visits from her mother and the trips to the Hall.

Motherhood was good. Norma was always smiling and her
big, green eyes searched her mother's face whenever Amy
looked down into the pools of emerald. She was beginning to
have hair; the family auburn bang was sprouting across the
middle of Norma's head.

"Isn't it odd," said Amy to her mother when she next visited.

"Just like your's," replied Alice. "I expect it will be curly too.
All the family seem to have inherited the Spanish locks."

Amy was getting a little bored with her evenings without
adult company, so she eventually told May that she would
consider going out sometimes. May had already experienced
the loneliness and belonged to the baby-sitting group, who
took turns in baby minding in the evenings. Her children
were aged twelve and ten, so she felt at ease if another
woman stayed with them whilst she went to the cinema or a
dance. Over a cup of tea, she suggested that Amy should join
the group and have a social life. At first Amy said it wasn't
necessary, having only thought about May and she doing
something together. She felt tempted, especially when she
recalled her American Airman who had called in.

When the next dance was announced, May suggested that
she baby-sat for Norma so that Amy could go along with

the other wives. Norma knew May better than anyone else, other than her mother, so Amy felt that she could leave her offspring without too much worry.

Amy dressed carefully and patted her hair into place. No need to paint the obligatory brown line on her calves as she carefully pulled on her nylons, adjusting the seam to ensure it was straight. She slipped her feet into her newly polished high-heeled shoes. She was ready!
She wondered if Guy would be there or if he had been sent on manoeuvres.

As she entered the dance hall, she glanced around and saw him standing near the bar with a group of other American men. He looked up and caught her eye.

"Good. You've made it!" he hailed her. "I hope you've got someone to look after that little mite."

"Oh. Yes," she smiled. "May's on duty."

"Come on then. Let's dance this jitter-bug."

He grabbed Amy's hand. It was a wonderful few hours for Amy. She had natural rhythm and was quick to learn new steps. Guy was an attentive partner and Amy found herself enjoying every moment of every dance with him. At the end of the evening, he vaguely suggested that he might drop in on her before the next dance.

"That would be lovely," replied Amy, although she thought he was being polite. He had certainly a lot of charm and good manners. She realised that these were the qualities that had attracted her to Bill when she first met him.

Excerpt from Amy's diary

February 1944
It was lovely to be able to let down my hair again. Guy and I danced every dance. We are really good together. It was different from turning Norma round and round in our living room. I'd forgotten how good it feels to dance with a man. Perhaps I shouldn't have let him kiss me though. THAT can be bad news!!! I'd better be careful, men aren't always what they seem.

Excerpt from Guy's diary

February 1944
She came! We had a marvellous time. Every dance. Bill doesn't
write much, but perhaps too busy. Might get killed . . . Holding
her at the end of the night was blissful. She even responded to
being kissed. Is this love? Feels more real than anything back
home.

It was not surprising that Guy began to fill Amy's
thoughts, especially when letters from William became
more infrequent and rather impersonal. He seemed unable
to show any feeling on paper. He would ask her direct
questions about his child or tell her about daily menus.
As men were not allowed to declare too much in letters,
and all letters were censored by the CO, the words were
stilted and Amy felt that his letters were more of an
obligation than a loving contact with his young wife and
new daughter. They had little to say to each other and Amy
had limited news to relate in her replies. She told William
about Norma's first steps and words and found little
anecdotes to relate that had been gleaned from her mother.
But conducting a marriage via letter proved to be very
problematic.

In March 1944 the Officers Advanced Training School was
set up. Many aircraft were operating from Cranwell now
and there were several serious accidents which affected
the wives as much as the personnel at the base. At their
weekly meetings, it became evident that young wives
were anxious about their men. Letters were few and far
between and were censored, so no one knew any details
of the whereabouts of menfolk or how the war was really
progressing.

The dances at the base continued throughout the year and
gave Amy something to look forward to beyond the home.
She often talked about the new dances that had been brought
over from The States when she and May had a cup of tea or
Camp coffee together.

Excerpts from Amy's diary

April 1944
Nothing from Bill for two whole months. Some of the women have had telegrams to tell them of the death of their husband or that they are missing—at least I haven't had that to worry about. Norma is growing up fast and she looks lovely in the jumper that ma brought over at Easter. Ma and pa gave me some material to make some bed coverlets—pink roses and lovely green swirls.
Looking forward to the dance on the base next month. Hope Guy is there. It was wonderful to be in his arms. Feeling someone next to you is a real joy, especially if it is someone you like. Really melted when he kissed me goodnight. Did I say that?!
May said that Guy had asked after me when I couldn't go to the dances, but that he danced with lots of girls during the evening . . .

Amy gained enormous joy from Norma, although she was showing the strong will of her father and could be quite difficult when she became stubborn.

There was speculation about the Second Front invading France during the next few months. Everyone believed that it would herald the end of the war.

Excerpts from Amy's diary

May 1944
There is a lot of aircraft noise and planes flying overhead. Expect it's something to do with the invasion of France. Perhaps the war will be over soon. Do hope so. Bill will be back and the Americans will leave I expect. Wonder how I'll feel?
Guy not at the dance this month. They say the men are really busy. Lots of us danced together because of the shortage of men. Not quite the same somehow.

June 1944
It happened. The newsreels are full of the exciting news. The landing craft swept up on the beaches and the men ran up through fighting and explosions everywhere. The Americans were involved but I couldn't see Guy anywhere. So many people must have been killed. But the end of the war should be getting closer. 5 years of war is enough for anybody.
Hope Guy's ok. I missed him at the dance and no one seems to know anything of his whereabouts.

The sun improved everyone's temper and Amy was generally feeling good in herself. She enjoyed May's friendship and the occasional social event that was organised at the base.

The women had made the baby sitting work well, organised their own 'card evenings' and decided that they should take it in turns to have a get together each week in the comfort of each others' houses. People let down their guard and realised that they must be friendly with those they met to ensure that they did not suffer from loneliness and make the most of the life they had.

Excerpts from Amy's diary

7th September 1944

Norma is One! She has five teeth and a cheery smile. Her hair has settled down, is auburn and will be curly. Ma and pa came over for the day on her birthday. They brought her a rocking horse that pa had made for her out of some spare wood and ma had baked a cake with a lovely candle in the middle. She was thrilled. May and her two lads came in for a piece of cake and a cuppa, so we had a good time.

It's the dance later in the month. It's ages since I saw Guy. Just not the same dances when he isn't there. Beginning to think about him a lot.

23rd September

Guy was at the dance. He has been involved with lots of war things—dropped troops and supplies for the Normandy landings and was doing the same at Market Garden in Holland. Says it's nerve racking but exciting at the same time. Lots of his mates have lost their lives but he thinks he was born under a lucky star—hope so. We had a glorious time. He walked me back to the house and gave me a wonderful goodnight kiss. Says he might come round if he gets any time. Hope so. He's SO lovely.

The excitement and anticipation of the October dance of 1944 filled her thoughts as she lay in bed each night, but she was slightly anxious about Guy as he had not visited as he had hinted he might when she saw him at the dance in September.

She need not have worried. Guy was again at the bar when she walked into the hall and he made a space for her to join him. They chatted but Amy felt that he was pre occupied.

When Guy announced that he had been put on stand-by duty, Amy's heart sank.

"I'll miss you," she whispered.

"I'll drop round on my off-duty, shall I?"

"Yes. Please do," she replied, wondering if he would turn up this time.

Excerpt from Amy's diary

October 1944
Oh God. Don't take him away. I don't know why, but he's become so important. He makes my legs go to jelly and I long to be with him. I never hear from Bill. Is he still alive? Letters are always so matter-of-fact and tell me nothing. I don't feel I know him any more. And then there's Guy. I know I'm in love with him. He has become SO special in so short a time—trust me!

By the end of the week, Amy was praying that Guy would visit. William was now only occasionally in her thoughts. She found that the maxim, 'out of sight, out of mind' fitted her temperament more that the one that assured others that 'absence makes the heart grow fonder'.

Excerpt from Guy's diary

October 1944
Have heard I've got to train for ops. Just when I'm beginning to be happy.
Will have to see Amy. Will take her a box of groceries.

Thirteen days after the dance, Amy answered the door to her new love.

"I shall be too busy to see you for a bit, so I decided to come over."

Amy stood aside and opened her home to the young American, who offered her a box. She took it through to the kitchen and put it on the table.

"Look in it," encouraged her American Airman.

There were tinned goods, butter, sugar, sweets, coffee, nylons and cigarettes.

Amy felt tears welling in her eyes and she bowed her head.

"Thank you for these. They'll be so useful."

Guy moved towards her and encircled her in his arms.

"You've been great," he whispered.

She lifted her head and he kissed her hungrily. Her feelings overwhelmed her. She knew that this time it was going to be different with Guy from the passionless encounters enjoyed by Bill and herself.

Norma was safely asleep in her bed in the second room, so she guided Guy to the bed that she had shared with her husband before the war.
He had never suggested that they took advantage of William being away, but the realisation that Guy may be leaving very soon, filled them both with a frantic desire to confirm their love for each other.

"I love you," whispered Guy as he pulled Amy towards him.

"Love you too," she replied.

Their kisses led to a feeling of longing that Amy had never experienced before. As Guy undresssed her and himself, they slipped under the bedclothes and their love found an outlet in the most deep form of sexual release that Amy had ever encountered.

Guy had to leave. He was due to report to his CO within the hour. He held Amy to him.

"Pray I don't get killed," he said.

Amy's tears rained onto his shoulder, which made him cry. They knew they loved each other and that it all could be futile. Guy dropped a final kiss on her forehead and ran to his jeep, roaring down the road without turning back.

Amy burst into fresh sobs. She knew she had found her soul mate.

What would become of their love?
What would happen to Bill?
How could she have been unfaithful to him when he was so far away?
How could she not have shown Guy how much she loved him before he went away?
What if anything happened to Guy?

Her questions were interrupted by a little voice.

"Mummy!"

Excerpt from Guy's diary

October 1944
My oh my. What love. She is an ANGEL.
We both cried. At least I go away, knowing that she loves me. I pray I live.

November 1944
Now know will be the lead navigator for the squadron when we go to drop reinforcements next time. Shall get the maps to study shortly. Gee whiz. Wish I could tell Amy, but doubt if I'll be able to see her before we go. Me and the guys'll celebrate Christmas big time, wherever we are, cos who knows what may happen.

Chapter 6   An Unexpected Joy

**It was December 1944 and there was still a war being waged
to save Britain from Nazi rule. The few air raids made little
effect on Amy as she had more personal worries.**

Excerpts from Amy's diary

December 1944
Oh God. The curse hasn't arrived AGAIN. When I'm not being
sick, I feel sick. Will have to go and see Dr. Grace soon. Fear the
worse . . . Good job Norma is a good little girl.

January 1945
HELP!
Sure enough. What am I going to do? Is it possible to love two
men at the same time? Guy has gone. He doesn't know. What
am I going to tell Bill? He'll never forgive me . . . I was lonely and
needed a bit of cheering up. Rash behaviour . . . I loved Guy—and
Bill? Am I going to pay . . .

Pregnant. A child created by a lover.
Pregnant. A baby made 'cause I love Guy.
Pregnant. A word once treasured above all other.
Pregnant. A word now uttered with a sigh.
Pregnant. We had once waited so long.
Pregnant. Norma's arrival; a cause for song.
The dances were fun, but I'll now pay the price
Of falling in love with someone as nice
As Guy—but he's gone away in a plane
Perhaps I'll not see or touch him again.
William away for a year—such a bore
Fighting away in this dreadful war,
Not seen our Norma; we'd waited for years,
Our life without babies meant so many tears,
I found I was pregnant after he'd gone
But he will be pleased that all is now done.
He's fighting this war in far, distant lands
We all will be safe in his capable hands.
But what shall I do? He may not accept
Another child with the one he's not met.

I'm scared; afraid that people may talk
I'll soon not be able to take a good walk.
A sister for Norma would be such a joy,
But it could be exciting to give birth to a boy.
I'll just have to breathe and then learn to wait,
Six more months, and I'll know my fate.

Here she was: a young woman of 30 with a small daughter,
a husband away with the RAF in India and an absent
lover from the local American base, who was the father
of the unborn baby she was carrying. Once the baby was
showing, she wondered how she was going to explain it to her
neighbours and family.

What was she going to write to Bill?
Should she tell Guy if she ever found out where he was?

Amy decided that no-one would know the name of the baby's
father and only if it became necessary would she confess her
pregnancy to her husband; after all, he could be killed.

Excerpts from Amy's diary

February 1945
Have decided to keep it quiet for a bit longer until I show. I'll tell
May next door. Wish I hadn't gone to the dances again. Guy was
lovely and made me feel special—just like Bill used to when we
went dancing at Sleaford. Poor Norma. How will she react to a
brother or sister.

In March, Amy asked May if she could talk to her. They met
for a cup of tea in May's kitchen. Amy could hardly speak.
After small talk about the weather, the neighbours and the
children, she eventually managed to tell May that she was
late with her period, had got over being sick every morning,
and knew she was pregnant.

She refused to say whose baby she was carrying, but May
guessed.

"I expect it's that Guy you've been with at the dances. I
shouldn't have encouraged you to go and enjoy yourself!"

When Amy did not answer, May told her to write to William.

"He'll kill me. We'd tried for a baby for years and he hasn't even seen Norma yet."

"Look. You've got to pull yourself together for everyone's sake. It would be best if you went to see the Welfare—you're not the only woman in this hole. Once you've seen her, you can tell your ma and pa. They'll help you."

She patted Amy's hand.

"And I'm here to give you a hand and a good talking to," she laughed.

"Thank you, May. You've always been kind to me. I'll try and stay calmer. Poor little Norma. It must have been funny for her seeing her mummy so poorly every morning."

"I expect you've given her lots of cuddles to make up for it," said May, in her no-nonsense way. "Now come on. Drink up and let's get back to normal. Let me know what's happening when you've seen the Welfare."

"Ok, May . . . Thanks again."

After her visit to May, Amy knew that her friend would support her and felt better and more able to handle the burden that she had carried for the last few months. She had few regrets. She and Guy had been in love and she was to bear his child as a testament to this love.

Excerpts from Amy's diary.

March 1945
May was lovely and gave me hope. She said I was to write and tell Bill. Oh dear . . .
Have posted letter to Bill. Still feeling a bit queasy but was like this with Norma. Must be another girl.
Also wrote to Ma and Pa. They won't be happy, although I expect Ma will do all she can—she's a good sort.
Have an appointment with doctor next month. Must ask her about the Welfare.
Have had a letter from Guy. He says he's had some frightening moments, but can't tell me where he is, so I can't write. Probably a

good job; he doesn't need to be saddled with the worry of being a father to a married woman's unborn child.
But I'm sure we loved each other.

April 1945
Ma and Pa came over to visit. Were pretty ok but not pleased that I wouldn't tell them the father's name. NO ONE will ever know—what's the point? If Guy comes home and we can have a life together it might be a different matter. Ma says she'll come down in July to be with me; what more could I ask?

Hitler killed himself in Berlin on 30th April 1945, which was followed by the German forces surrendering to the Allies in Italy on May 2nd and in Germany on May 7th. Everyone rejoiced. The 8th May was declared as VE Day(Victory in Europe) and there was much celebration throughout the regions, including at RAF Cranwell.

A huge dance was held, but Amy decided to be the baby sitter for the circle of mothers, as she could not bear the thought of dancing again without Guy or even Bill. Anyway, at the beginning of the month, she had received a letter from her husband, who was still in India. She had been forced to confess that there would be a second child when he returned.

May 1945
Letter from Bill. Not happy. Says I've a choice . . . him or the baby. Call THAT a choice? He made the point that we had tried for years for a baby and he hasn't even seen Norma. Wondered AGAIN if she was his . . . which she is. He says he's cried and had sleepless nights over my 'betrayal'. All about him as usual!! Says it would be impossible for him to act as a father to a child that is not his so I have to surrender my 'second born' if I want him back to look after Norma. Will talk to the doc tomorrow. There's another girl on the base who has had her baby adopted through Welfare, so will try to go down that route.
Wish I could tell Guy about our baby. I miss him SO much.

June 1945
It's all set up. Someone will visit me next week.
Guy is missing. Presumed killed in action. He'll never know about our baby. Feel DREADFUL. Don't think I have any more tears left in me. Why did it have to be him who was killed? I have nothing of him, except this baby—am enormous, so I expect the baby can't be far off—and the wonderful memories.

The truth is hard. May MUST realise she guessed right as I nearly cried in front of her when I heard of Guy's crew going missing. She never says much—a good friend.

Met up with Joy who had a baby adopted last month. She says she HAD to go down that route as her husband has refused to have him when he returns and they have three others. She says the hurt passes and she has found that if she keeps herself over busy she can almost forget . . . Who knows what the future holds.

In many ways I don't want to forget. BUT, I have to be strong as I still have Norma and I must make sure she is ok.

Amy went round to tell May about the arranged adoption. She was very supportive and told her that it was probably the best thing for everyone concerned. Over a cup of strong tea, which May regarded as a cure for all troubles, May consoled her friend.

"It'll be hard for you. I'd hate to be in your shoes. Don't think I could give up my child."

"What else can I do? Bill won't have it in the house when he returns. I shall tell him that he doesn't need to know anything about the father because he's been killed anyway."

Amy dissolved into tears. May put her arms round her neighbour and let her cry. Eventually she calmed down and May made her promise to hold things together and get on with her life for Norma's sake.

Amy's mother came to stay at the beginning of July. Norma thought it was wonderful to have her grandmother around, especially as her Mummy was always having to rest because she was so fat. Norma knew that the baby was making her fat, but was not sure that it should interfere with playtime with her mother. However, Grandma was a great substitute as she was full of fun for someone so old. Norma organised her grandmother and Amy was able to get some much-needed rest. With beautiful weather, Amy's mother was able to take her little granddaughter for walks in and around the base, so the days passed quickly.

The new baby was delivered in the middle of July. Amy's labour began in the middle of the night and as dawn broke, a tiny girl emerged into the world. She had wisps of

red hair, like all the family, which broke Amy's heart as she knew she would have to surrender this tiny creature. But how could she let Norma grow up without her father?

Her mind was in turmoil.

The baby was a good child, who responded to the love that she poured out to her. Norma was becoming more difficult to cajole or amuse.
Amy knew that her affair with Guy was to cost her dear.

July 1945
The baby is beautiful and so good. Norma loves her and wants to hug and kiss her. Sister Willett of Welfare has found a nice childless couple for her. Bill is due home in a few months . . . perhaps he'll change his mind when he sees her. Have told Norma that her Daddy is coming home and I think she understands. Mother has warned me that life will not be easy. She was a godsend and having her around made things so much more bearable. Norma loved it and doesn't seem to have suffered from the experience of becoming a big sister. In fact, she has blossomed. We both missed Ma when she returned to the Hall. Expect Pa was pleased to have her back. He says I hogged her for too long—think he's joking!!

It was a good summer, with sun and warmth for days on end, which meant that Amy was able to walk the baby and her small daughter round the camp grounds. The garden was a haven for the small family and provided shelter from the rest of the world when Amy felt that people were talking about her.

Norma grew into a beautiful child. She spent hours running around in the garden, making mud pies whenever it had rained, stuffing sultanas into her mouth when her mother was baking, swinging on the swing that they had managed to erect in the garden, playing with the toys and the children down the road. She loved her new sister and helped her mother at bath times, often pretending that Joanna was her baby!
Joanna Dawn (to reflect the time of her birth) thrived in the love and attention showered on by her mother and sister. She developed a ready smile, unaware of what her future may hold.

Chapter 7   Heartbreak

Amy's second child was the spitting image of her mother, which made Amy sad, as she had hoped to have a child that reminded her of Guy. As she had already signed papers to give her up, it was probably better that Joanna was not a mirror image of her father—that could make parting even more difficult.

War still continued with Japan until the surrender on 14th August, which resulted in VJ Day (victory over Japan) on the following day. The excitement about the end of war was infectious and people celebrated in the streets. It was a time for everyone to be contemplating the joys of being alive.

For Amy, it was a time of stress and fear of the unknown. She dreaded William's return. Memories of his temper and lack of humour haunted her and she knew he would not forgive her for her affair with Guy, although he would probably pretend to the world that he was magnanimous about it. She found it impossible to enter into the spirit of victory, although she knew it was for the benefit of the country. William had been irascible with no good cause so now that he had a reason, Amy knew that he would make her suffer.

Amy had made all the necessary arrangements to surrender Joanna. Her life seemed to be shattering like glass before her eyes. She was going to have to lose her final link with the love of her life. Joanna had been so good and beautiful and had epitomised her great love for Guy.

Norma was becoming a challenging child, but at least she belonged to her husband—not that he seemed sure of that fact. How would William react? He would be home by the end of the month and Amy feared for herself and *both* children.

2nd September 1945
Good job I was there. Norma decided that Joanna should sample the sultanas. I was making a cake to welcome home William—he's expected in a couple of days. Shame he couldn't be here for

Norma's second birthday. As I turned round from the counter, Joanna was choking. Norma looked alarmed and said, "Baby wants stanas. They're nice. Norma likes them." I managed to get the sultanas out of Joanna's mouth and she started to cry. "Baby likes stanas too." I explained that she may do, but she is too young and has to have the food mummy gives her. Norma promised not to give her anything else. Will have to keep a closer eye on things. I know it's only love for her little sister that Norma feels. God. How will she react when we lose our little maiden? Can't bear to think of it.

7thSeptember 1945

Bill is back. He is thrilled with Norma but adamant that the baby goes. Insisted that we celebrated Norma's birthday as it was so near to his arrival home. He made a huge fuss of her, making it doubly obvious that he was ignoring Joanna. Norma even tried to involve her—after all, she feels J is just as much her baby as mine. Norma finds Daddy difficult but she'll get used to him in time, hopefully. He's so hard and indifferent to me—not a bit like Guy. Can't feel the same intensity of love with him. Impossible to put Guy right out of my mind and I have to shut myself in the lav when the waves of despair come over me and I have to cry. It's a different situation entirely, but Guy can't come back and Norma needs her father. My little baby has to go. It doesn't matter how I plead, Bill is firm and won't consider keeping her. He knows she's a good child but he says he needs to give all his love to Norma to make sure she grows up like him—even if she might not be his. I KNOW she's his—I didn't look at anyone until I met Guy. I shall never forget those wonderful times with him; he was everything a girl could want. No wonder I couldn't have him—it was too perfect. Now I have to make the best of it for the family's sake. As mother says, God moves in mysterious ways.

It was a difficult time at first for William and Amy when the former returned. He had to become accustomed to this mother of a toddler who he had fathered but never seen. There was also the wife, who seemed to be a stranger to him. The wife with a baby who was the result of a liaison with an American Airman. He did not know what to say to her. Amy tried to understand that he had endured an horrific time. He was reluctant to share his experiences with her or any other person who had not seen war at first hand.

Amy was pleased when William went into work as it meant that she could spend time with the girls. She was only too aware that time was running out and that her precious baby was to be taken away. She tried to make the most of the last few days with Joanna. Norma was too small to realise that she would lose her baby sister, and was delighted to spend so much time playing and walking.

Excerpt from Amy's diary.

September 28th
The lady from the Welfare will be here tomorrow. Feel absolutely frightened to death. Whatever she says, I am NOT going to mention Joanna's father. He gave his life, so his memory is not going to be harmed by me in any way. If he'd lived, who knows what might have happened? Oh, if only. It's going to be so hard, but as ma said, I've got to do this for Norma's sake. My poor little mite. Surely they'll find a good home for her. I know I'll think of her every day. Hope Bill will be better once she has gone. I know it's difficult for him seeing her in the house—a constant reminder that I was unfaithful. Will I ever learn to live with the guilt? Somehow, Joanna's existence made it alright. It's only since Bill's been home that I've felt any sadness—not even that really, but sorry that I've hurt so many people. Oh Guy. I really loved you.

On September 29th, Sister Willett visited in order to take the final details in preparation for an adoption. William was working in the hangars, although he probably could have delegated the task, so Amy was alone when the visitor arrived. Amy found it easier without William by her side as he had been very difficult about Joanna still being in the house when he came back after the last meeting. She was hoping that once the baby had gone, she, William and Norma could begin to build a new life together.

Amy read the questions typed on the form and handed it back to Sister Willett saying,

"Please will you fill this in if I give you the answers?"

The form asked for the mother's name, address, date and place of the child's birth and the authorisation that an adoption was what was required. Amy answered everything until she was asked to supply the 'Name of father'.

"I'd rather not say," said Amy.

"But I think you have to give a name."

"No," replied a determined Amy. "There's no need. He died before the baby was born."

"Did he know you were pregnant?"

"Does that matter? Her father died for a good cause and I don't want his name sullied by being shown on the record of an illegitimate birth."

"What does your husband think?"

"He's left it to me. As long as the baby is taken away, he'll be happy. He wants his own family and we shall have other children for Norma to play with."

"O.K. I'll try and make sure that the authorities will accept your wishes."

After a cup of tea and a piece of Amy's renowned fruit cake, Sister Willett left, explaining that she would return on October 26th to collect the baby in order to take her to her adoptive parents.

October 4th.
Oh God, please help me. My baby is being taken away. I can't bear it. She's too little to go and live away from me. How can I stop it? No child should lose its mother, just because of a mistake—perhaps if Bill had been more loving when he was here I wouldn't have fallen in love with someone else. He can't take the love of Guy and me away even if he manages to have my little one put with new people. Sister Willett says they can't have a family, so perhaps they'll look after her really well. I'll have to be a good mother to Norma to make up for everything. I wonder if she'll remember her baby sister. What a hellish situation to be in. No one could possibly understand how I feel—but I know May does her best. Must keep busy and love J every day so that I'll be able to think of her smell and her features when she's gone. Why oh why can't Bill change his mind. Please help me God.

Coming home from war had many problems for the men and when William returned from work later in the week, he was in a terrible mood. One of his men had spoken when he was giving information out and he had 'lost it'. Everyone forgave the incident and blamed the after effects of the war, but Amy knew that the men had seen his true nature. Needless to say, William did not mention the incident. May heard it from her husband and she told it to Amy in the hope that it would make her neighbour feel better.

May had always been supportive of Amy and recognised that William was not as easy-going and thoughtful as her own man. She therefore had some sympathy with her friend. In fact, she felt slightly responsible as she had encouraged Amy to go to the dances—had she not gone she would not have met Guy and then there would have been no baby to be making her life problematical . . . May knew that her friendship would be needed even more, once baby had been taken from her mother.

Other girls on the base had suffered and all seemed to come through the other side eventually, except for Elizabeth James, who had left her husband and gone back to her parents because she was at breaking point. May steeled herself for the inevitable tears and trauma when Amy surrendered her child to the Welfare.

True to her word, on the morning of October 26th, Sister Willett knocked on the door. William was at home and showed her into the front room. The baby was wrapped in a shawl sleeping in the pram and a pile of baby clothes was neatly stacked on a chair. Norma sat on her mother's lap, sucking her thumb and looking bewildered.

"There's a problem, Mrs. Jackson. The authorities insist that you give the name of the father."

"No."

"Just give his surname. There will be so many complications if you don't."

Amy remained resolute and refused to speak.

"Put Barkus," suggested William, "he was obviously willing," he smirked.

"Will that be alright, Mrs. Jackson?"

"Of course it will," interrupted William. "Let's get this done with so that we can get on with our own lives."

Amy wasn't sure if she had ever known Guy's surname anyway. She glanced across at her second daughter who was unaware that she was to be uprooted. What could she do? William was going to be firm and who could blame him?

She nodded in response to Sister Willett's enquiring look. She was unable to speak and hugged her older daughter to her.

"O.K.then," said Sister Willett, standing up and putting the documents away. "I'll put these clothes in my holdall and take the baby to the station for her journey. You know that you must NOT try to contact her or her new family, don't you?"

Amy nodded.

"Of course not," assured William, as he took the baby out of the pram and placed her in Sister's arms.

"She'll be better off with people who'll really love her," he added.

"There'll be the formal meetings in London which you must attend. You'll be asked if you have changed your mind about allowing the adoption."

"There'll not be any change of heart, I assure you," replied William

Amy felt her eyes welling with tears and she shoved her face into the top of Norma's head. Norma knew that things were not right.

"Kiss baby," she said, raising her arms to her father.

Sister Willett eased the baby towards the lips of the toddler, who planted a kiss on the baby's forehead whilst she exchanged looks with Amy, who sat on the sofa alone, with tears streaming down her face and clutching her body.

"We'll see you out," said William, turning his daughter away from her mother and walking into the hallway.

"I'll be in touch," she smiled at the bereft mother.

"Goodbye," she added to William as she walked past him and made her way to her car.

Sister Willett placed the baby in the rear seat and wedged her in with the holdall of clothes and her work bag. Turning the key, pulling out the choke, pushing the starter, releasing the handbrake, engaging the clutch and accelerating, Sister Willett made her way to the station. The train to Grantham left at 11.40. The baby had hardly stirred and at this stage was oblivious of the changes taking place in her young life.

"Where's Joanna?" asked Norma of her father on his return to the sitting room.

"She's gone on her holidays", replied William.

"Want to go too."

"No," said her mother. "We'll have a nice day out at the weekend when daddy isn't working."

Amy took her daughter onto her knee and covered her head with kisses.

"That's enough," snapped William, taking Norma into his own arms.

"Let's go to the rec and play ball."

Amy was left, bereft and deserted. She sobbed uncontrollably and knew that life would never be the same again.

Amy flung herself on to the bed. She had made such a mess of her life. Handing a baby over to a Welfare Officer was something that she had never envisaged.

How could she have thought that her life would be unaffected by the events of 1944? Why had she not realized that her husband would react in this way?

She felt that her heart would break.

How would this predicament affect her precious first born? Would she miss her new sister? It need not have been like this, if only . . .

Why did it have to be *him* that had returned safely?

Why was she being made to feel guilty, humiliated, dirty?

He had taken their small daughter out, away from the house of shame and heartache.

Would they come back? Would she lose both her babies on the same day?

Chapter 8   A New Beginning.

Amy had her treasured possessions in an old shoe box, which lived in the bottom of the wardrobe. Amongst them was a curl from her own head of hair, a curl from Norma's, letters from her mother and those from Bill when he was on war duty. Hidden amongst these letters was the only precious letter that she had received from Guy, and her diary (which she prayed William never found). It was to this that she turned her tear-stained face and wrecked spirit.

October 27th 1945
My baby has gone. Have cried all day and all night. I know my eyes are red and swollen. May had Norma for me but I'll have to sort myself out pretty soon—Bill doesn't have any sympathy. He'll be glad to start over. Only May seems to understand. I might suggest I take Norma over to ma and pa's for a day or two and see how they think I ought to go on.

For days Amy wept and tried desperately to keep things together. Her life had been shattered; she had lost her younger child but she had to continue for Norma's sake.

William Jackson was aware that he had treated his wife harshly. He knew she had been a good wife to him for many years before the war and that it had been difficult for her when he was away. Life in the air force had been trying for him too. He had been made a flight sergeant and was highly thought of initially. At first he had missed his wife and home—and then Amy's image had begun to disappear into the ether as he became immersed in his work.

He knew war had changed him.

This did not make things any easier for him. He found it almost impossible to forgive his wife her affair and although he realised that she had been lonely and the dances had enabled her to forget her worries, he felt that she had destroyed any faith he had in her. He knew he was curt with May next door but he thought she should not have encouraged Amy to go to the dances. On the other hand, *she* had been able to stay faithful to Stanley.

His thoughts became a shambles and he decided that he must again immerse himself into his work in order to stay sane. On good days, he remembered that he was the father of a precious daughter who could become the focus of his attention.

May was a wonderful friend to Amy and gave her encouragement and reasons for carrying on. She was always ready to lend a listening ear and ply her with drinks and biscuits, or have Norma for a few hours so that she could shop in Sleaford or clean the house. She appreciated that Amy felt she had to be doubly clean in the house or twice as domesticated as everyone else in order to ensure that William was kept sweet. News of his temper had become the talk of the base, so May knew she had to be protective of her neighbour.

Sometimes, Amy needed to talk about Joanna, but she never mentioned Guy—and May decided that she must not divulge her suspicions to anyone. After all, Guy had given his life for the country and that must be the main reason to keep his name away from the other people on the base. No one else had mentioned him, so she kept her own counsel.

Without May's support, Amy would have suffered unbearably. Her mother was rarely able to visit as she was getting on in years and the travelling was too difficult and long for her to endure. Her father did not know the right words of comfort to use anyway.

There were hundreds of illegitimate babies born to married women throughout the world during the war and many of the mothers found themselves forced to surrender the tiny baby when their spouse returned from the Front. No one can know how dreadful it was for these women who found themselves in this predicament; Amy was by no means alone.

Chapter 9   Fulfilment

Patrick Henderson had lived in Stamford, in the south of
the large county of Lincolnshire, for all his 39 years. He had
enjoyed a happy childhood, under the regime of his strict
mother whose father had produced a 'baker's dozen', (which
was fitting as he was a baker in a small village to the west
of Stamford). Patrick's own father worked in the Foundry
of the local engineering factory and when Patrick was
fourteen he joined his father there. He had received a private
education in the small school run by Miss Hill until he was
ten, but had learned little of use to his later career and was
very aware that his spelling skills were basic.

At the age of six, Patrick's days of being an only child ended
when his cousin, whose parents had been found gassed in
their tiny cottage whilst their young son was at school, joined
the family. No one spoke overtly of the disaster, but Patrick
gathered from the snippets that he overheard that there were
money worries and that his uncle and aunt could not face the
idea of the bailiffs moving in, although they had shown little
consideration for their son. No doubt his uncle had known
in his heart that his sister and her husband would give a
home to Dave and bring him up with their own son; which,
fortunately, proved to be good for both of the boys.

Mrs. Henderson often prepared a meal for her extended
family on a Sunday, when her parents could spare a few
hours away from bread making in their own village. It
was customary for the bake-house in Stamford to offer its
oven for the cooking of large Yorkshire puddings if people
booked a place beforehand. Patrick and Dave had the
responsibility for taking the swirling batter in its tin down
to the bake-house where they waited for it to be cooked
and then hurried home with it before it got cold. One day,
on the way to the bake-house, the boys forgot to heed their
'mother's' warning and began to swing the tin backwards
and forwards. They then decided to skip along and sing a
song they had recently learned together from an uncle who
had visited. Neither of the boys realised that the swings

were becoming too vigorous and the pudding mixture was beginning to encroach on the sides of the tin. With one huge swing of joy, the liquid burst its banks like the River Welland onto the dirty road. Both boys knew that 'mother' would be furious if there was no Yorkshire with the Sunday roast. They proceeded to do what every small boy would do (in order to preserve himself from the wrath of an adult), they scooped as much of the mixture back into the tin with their palms and a stray leaf that lay handily nearby. They then went on to the bake-house and acted as if nothing untoward had happened. Patrick admitted in later life that the pudding was an unusual colour, but, as far as he knew, no one had been any the wiser about its adventure.

When Patrick was nine, his mother gave birth to a tiny daughter. Patrick's duties around the house were doubled when his mother became ill shortly afterwards. He loved his baby sister dearly and was very conscious of his mother's plight, so did everything with a good grace. He missed his cousin when Dave was sent to live with Aunt Ethel in Ketton. An extra child was too much for his mother to cope with and Ethel's children had already left home.

At the age of ten, Patrick transferred to the local primary school and charmed teachers with his good manners and natural respect for authority. The Hendersons were Christian people who could be seen regularly in the congregation of St. Michael's Church in the old market town. The parents passed on their values and faith to their children, which stood them in good stead during their lives.

Patrick's parents decided that he should serve an apprenticeship, so at the age of fourteen, he embarked on his journey towards becoming a Pattern Maker. As he was precise—if not slightly pedantic—he was acclaimed for his work, although he refused the chance of becoming a Foreman because he felt he would not be able to bear the responsibility. A gentle, humble man, he won the hearts of many, including Pamela James, who had come to Stamford from her birth town in Warwickshire to live with her eldest sister and brother-in-law, after the death of her father when she was a mere thirteen. Her elder sister had died of TB the previous year so life had become difficult in the home and her mother was forced to find further employment in order to make ends meet. As Nell, her sister, had no children from her marriage to Albert, it seemed fitting for young Pamela to move up to them; for the immediate future, at least. Pamela settled well until she was eighteen, when she saw a notice in the magazine that her sister read, advertising a post as governess/nursemaid to two small children whose parents were going to Jersey. She applied and was interviewed by the Hollands, was accepted and set sail for Jersey with her new family in 1925.

Pamela enjoyed two wonderfully happy years before Mr. Holland was moved back to the British Isles and the children were sent to Boarding School, so her services were no longer needed. Pamela returned to the haven of her sister's home, where there was a new baby in the family. She enjoyed 'mothering' her nephew, but knew that she must find employment to sustain a life style that she had experienced in Jersey. A position came up in a shoe shop, where she met her friend, Madeleine, who was to remain a staunch ally for the rest of her life.

Pamela was always very proud of the fact that she had fitted Mrs. Sergeant (Sir Malcolm's mother) with her shoes and was left a small legacy by her when she died. Pamela moved to work in a grocer's shop later on. Her previous Manager was intently jealous of her inheritance from Mrs. Sergeant and had made life uncomfortable for her. It was at the grocery that she met Patrick when he called in for produce one Saturday morning.

They were soon courting and Patrick proposed and was accepted in 1928.

—0—

"Let's cycle to Southam at the weekend," said Pamela.

"Want to show your sister your ring, eh?" teased Patrick.

"Well yes," she admitted, "and I want to know when it'll be the best time for ma to come up for the wedding."

"I'm sure she'll fit in with any plans we make. Don't worry about the Southam lot. We all get on so well, it'll be a great occasion."

Patrick and Pamela had regularly cycled to Southam at weekends and holiday times. These trips were an opportunity for Pamela to see her mother and siblings. Patrick looked forward to them as much as his fiancé. Pamela's sister Rose and her husband always ensured they had a good time together. Fred was a jazz pianist with a group who played at The Craven Arms Hotel every Saturday, so the four young people enjoyed themselves dancing and singing until the early hours. Pamela's mother often joined them as she was a 'live-wire' for her age and was delighted that her two daughters had found such happiness.

As Patrick had predicted, the family were pleased about the forthcoming wedding and promised to attend the event, if their business commitments allowed.

Pamela walked on air and her smile stretched from Southam to Stamford. Her love for Patrick was deeper than she had ever imagined a love could be. Fortunately, he felt an all-consuming love for her. His only worry was that they would be forced to live with his parents until a council house became available. He then intended to save as much as possible so that they could purchase their own home.

Pamela's mother suggested that her daughter spent a few days with her before the wedding, which was arranged for Easter Monday of 1929. During this week, Pamela decided to write to her beloved Patrick.

My own darling Patrick,
I am still trying to do my best to write this so that when it reaches you it will be readable. I hope you will not have any trouble that way. Darling one I am feeling so excited at the thought of Easter which is drawing very near to us now. I hope and pray you will never regret the step we are about to take together. I want to be your own, your all, your wife, to love always in the years to come. May they be long and many and never regretted.
Ever your own sweetheart & Wife to be, Pamela x

Pamela and Patrick were married at the Parish Church of All Saints in The Square on Easter Monday, which happened to be All Fool's Day. Pamela chose a fashionable calf-length, A-line white wedding dress. She wore white lace gloves, a veil with imitation flowers and pearls which sat around her face, white satin 2" heeled shoes with a bow and strap and she carried a bouquet of Spring flowers and orchids. Round her throat, she wore a single row of pearls, a treasured present from Patrick. He wore a smart striped, dark suit, with the obligatory white handkerchief peeping from the top pocket, a silver-grey tie, an orchid buttonhole and highly polished black shoes. They made a very handsome couple.

Appropriate to the day, Albert, who was Patrick's best man, forgot to pay the vicar and he also filled their umbrella with confetti, which poured all over the honeymooners in Sheringham, Norfolk, two days after the wedding. The young couple rode the storm well and even earned a free drink from the people they stayed with for Bed & Breakfast.

Pamela and Patrick were very happy, despite the necessity of living in the front room of Patrick's parents' house. Pamela found her in-laws slightly trying and never quite forgave her mother-in-law coming into their bedroom on their first night back from honeymoon, in order to plant a kiss on her son's cheek!

By 1934, the young Hendersons had put down a deposit on a three-bedroom house on The Drift; a house that Pamela had only dreamed about.

Patrick made cupboards in the kitchen and a lean-to in the garden where Pamela could keep her dolly tub and mangle, which were used on wash days. He then drew up plans for a glass addition to the side of the house, which they later furnished with a table and chairs and used it for dining on pleasant, sunny days or as a workspace for woodwork projects.

Patrick had become a Church Warden at All Saints Church in the town and he was kept busy with the demands of the position, whilst Pamela enjoyed the status that it brought to them.

Their happiness had been marred by only one thing: no family.
Both Pamela and Patrick had seen doctors and had tests to investigate the lack of a baby. Despite drugs and relaxation sessions no baby had appeared. They decided to adopt. They had approached an adoption agency but unfortunately, the outbreak of war delayed their plans. They decided to live life to the full and wait to see what it offered them.

They were too old to serve in any of the armed forces but Patrick joined the Auxiliary Fire Service so that he could continue at his daytime job, which was in a reserved occupation. Pamela stayed at the Grocer's shop and often spent nights at the fire station, unless she was required to do anything by the Red Cross for whom she volunteered, despite her fear of illness and injury. She knew she had to do her bit for the war!

Pamela's mothering instincts were satisfied by the frequent visits of her sister's youngest daughter, Betty. Her weekend visit to them became a week's visit, which then developed into a month's visit and eventually, six months of every year was spent in Stamford whilst Pamela's sister and husband ran a business in Southam. Patrick shared Pamela's joy of their niece. Patrick decided that as there was to be no baby of their own, perhaps Rose and Fred would let them adopt Betty. However, when this idea was put to them, Fred resisted it and insisted that his daughter spent more time at home.

After the war had ended, Patrick and Pamela were anxious that their application to become adopters would be over-looked, but they were thankful that they had survived the war and most of their friends, like them, were still enjoying life. Needless to say the Second World War had produced many unwanted babies. The Hendersons were delighted when they received a letter at the beginning of June 1945 from The Church Welfare telling them that a child had been found for them if they were still interested in adoption.

Pamela was over the moon, but Patrick had reservations.

"How do we know it won't be a child from a service man from overseas?" he asked Pamela.

"We don't. But we do know that there is a child who has no one to call its own unless we have it."

Patrick could see that Pamela was desperate and, as he could refuse her nothing, he agreed that Pamela could contact the adoption authority.
A telegram arrived.

A Sister Willett would be visiting them the following Wednesday.
Patrick asked for the afternoon off from work and they replied that they would be available for a visit.

Pamela baked a fruit cake so that she could offer something with a cup of tea and spent the Tuesday cleaning their house from top to bottom so thoroughly that any one would have thought that Royalty were visiting rather than a lady from The Church Welfare.

Pamela felt that her heart would burst with pleasure and anxiety and poor Patrick's stomach worked overtime because he was so nervous.

What if Sister Willett thought they were:
too old
too set in their ways
too old fashioned
too wrapped up in each other
too out of touch with modern ideas
too . . .

The list was endless and caused them both sleepless nights.

They need not have worried. There were so many war babies who needed parents and insufficient people prepared to give their homes to tiny unwanted mites who only needed love.

Patrick was slightly alarmed when Sister Willett told them that the child they had been allocated was of mixed parentage, but when he saw a photograph of the little girl in question his fears were instantly allayed. After a number of visits from Sister Willett of The Church Welfare Society, all was approved and the adoption was underway.

The Hendersons were to become parents in six weeks from her last visit. They were advised to warn their family and friends of the expected arrival. Until this point, they had not discussed their intentions of becoming parents with anyone except their vicar, who had acted as their sponsor with The Church Welfare Society and been involved before the war had changed everyone's plans.

Patrick thought his parents might be difficult. He wondered if they would accept a child who was not blood-related. Pamela told him that she thought it would be easier now that his sister had presented them with a grandson. She felt that her own mother would accept a child as she had offered to baby-sit for them when she moved up to Stamford, if ever they became parents. Patrick's sister and her husband would be supportive as would her sisters and her oldest friend from work. Pamela was suitably sanguine. Their vicar was delighted for them and encouraged them to bring their new daughter to church as soon as possible so that she could become part of the congregation.

So, the bleak railway platform at Grantham on the 26th of the month was to be the start of a new life for these two excited people. It was a pleasant October day when Pamela and Patrick made their way from the beautiful market town of Stamford in order to collect a very special package from someone they had met earlier in the year. They sat in the waiting room in front of a roaring log fire along with other travellers who were waiting for trains from other parts of the country.

The train from Lincoln was announced. It was due on Platform 2, so they headed out across the bridge to await its arrival.

"I'm scared," confessed Pamela.

"Well don't be. It's our chance of a life time," reassured her husband, who had similar feelings.

Then the train was upon them. A dainty lady, dressed in a grey coat and carrying bags and a white bundle emerged from a carriage, aided by a polite gentleman who raised his hat on departure.

Recognising the excited couple, she approached them and carefully handed over her charge.

"Here is your new baby. I do hope your lives together will be rich and happy."

Patrick took the bundle from her and Pamela picked up the bags that went with their gift; for this was how they saw this dear baby. They had hardly exchanged a few words before Patrick turned and said,
"That's our train home being announced."

Sister Willett hugged Pamela and shook Patrick by the hand saying,
"I'll visit in a couple of weeks when you have settled into a routine."

The Hendersons boarded the train. By this time their gift had realised things were different and had started to cry.

"It's so difficult travelling with children isn't it!" commented a gentleman who was already seated in the carriage.

Patrick agreed, as though he had done travelling with children many times before, which made his wife smile.

The first night was sleepless for all concerned. Pamela was not only excited, but rather anxious (despite having been a children's nanny in a former life). Her husband fussed endlessly, trying to make sure that the little baby of 3 months was comfortable, and the latter fretted for her mother who was miles away in RAF Cranwell.

However, with the love showered on her, the baby soon settled well with her new parents. Sister Willett was delighted when she visited to find the little girl looking happy. She was obviously being well cared for, both physically and emotionally. Pamela and Patrick were over the moon with their bundle of joy and, despite the neighbour's snide comment of, "Now your troubles will begin", were determined that all would go well.

The ready smile and the pretty face of the new arrival soon wooed the grandparents. Patrick's sister and husband were delighted that their son would now have a cousin to grow up with. Pamela's niece, Betty, who had shared their lives for many years whilst her own parents tried to run a business, was thrilled with her tiny cousin. She readily became a surrogate mother being seventeen and ripe for motherhood.

Stamford soon learned of the beautiful baby that The Hendersons had been given through the church and most people shared the happiness of the immediate family. Everyone prayed that all would go smoothly in the crucial three months ahead.

No one need have worried.

William was not going to change his mind, he could never accept another man's child. Meetings were arranged by Church Welfare to give the opportunity for birth parents to review their decision in the presence of the adopting parents. Amy was unable to do anything about the situation. William had even refused to accompany her to the meetings about Joanna, so her mother came along, holding on to her hand as though they had been bereaved. After the first meeting in London Amy comforted herself in the knowledge that she liked the people who were adopting her second child. She would concentrate on building up her relationship with her husband and making a good home for her firstborn.

The second meeting saw Patrick's brother-in-law accompany him, (Joanna had only just recovered from bronchitis and still needed Pamela to look after her). The third meeting between the birth mother, grandmother and the adoptive

**parents went reasonably well and the baby was legally
adopted in February 1946.**

Patrick's diary

February 1946
Joanna Dawn Jackson. Born July 14 1945.
Grantham. Oct.26 1945. 3 months 12 days
London Mother Dec 11th 1945 *(Reference to an official meeting with
Joanna's birth mother)*
Bronchitis Jan 5th. Doctor on 8th 1946
(Stan) Mother Jan 31st 1946 *(Reference to an official meeting with the birth
mother, accompanied by Patrick's brother-in-law)*
London Mother Feb 25th 1946 *(Final official meeting with the birth mother)*
Legally adopted 27 Feb 1946 Town Hall—Joanna Doreen Henderson

**Pamela secretly wondered how the mother of her lovely
child was coping, for they had been told of the circumstances
of the birth. Pamela had been thankful that she had not
had to endure separation from Patrick during the war, his
being a reserved occupation. She could well appreciate the
loneliness that it must have meant for any young woman. She
was determined that she would never say anything negative
about Joanna's mother and would instil good values into the
little child who now belonged to them.**

Pamela's notes in an address book:

Fetched Joanna from Sister Willets October 26th. (Friday)
Cut first tooth Easter Sunday April22nd (9 months)
Crawled on bot 9 months
Standing up 10 ½ months
Walking 13months (10 teeth)
Horrified to see an auburn bang across her head; good job I love her.
Saying TA-TA & Baba 16months

Patrick's diary

First tooth EasterSunday 21April 1946
1 year old 14 July
Hymunised Aug 15 1946 1st time
Hymunised Sept 13th 1946 2nd time.
Applied to adopt another child.

Lovely red hair which curls. And green eyes. A little buty.

November 1947. Application been accepted. Pam very excited. It'll mean overtime to make ends meet, but will be good for Joanna.

Full set of teeth Jan 10th 1948

Freda's baby born Sun 11th Jan 1948 8lbs 3ozs. Brother for Dennis.

Feb 21st 1948 Whooping cough. No chance of adopting another child now. Been put at the bottom of the list. Will be too old by the time we get to the top. Pam doesn't seem too disappointed . . .

We shall be a small, happy family. All our eggs in one basket.

Chapter 10　　　A Small Happy Family

Joanna was bright, happy, and determined. When the Doctor was visiting at one time, Pamela mentioned that her young daughter appeared to be strong willed.

"That's good," replied Dr. Chase. "You need a good spirit to live in this changing world. She'll go far and you'll be able to rejoice in her success if you direct her into the right path."

The Hendersons were gentle people with good values and encouraged Joanna to befriend others, enjoy animals, take responsibilities, play hard and work hard. Patrick, himself, was a hard-working pattern maker in the local factory, he worked long hours from Tuesday to Thursday and Saturday mornings for many years, but he made time for his new family whenever possible.

He shared his wife's enthusiasm for parenthood. He played with his little daughter (even made a snowman in the snows of 1947) and his talent with wood and materials meant Joanna had beautiful tailored coats with velvet collars and cuffs, as well as a many-roomed dolls' house with precise miniature furniture in every room.

Pamela revelled in her new role as mother and encouraged her daughter as much as possible in her development.

The Henderson's neighbours were an elderly couple who originated from Bow, London. Their daughter was moved out from her home in London, to Stamford, for her confinement in 1945 and gave birth to a daughter at the end of July. The Hendersons were delighted to know that there was a ready-made friend in their neighbour's granddaughter. Many happy hours were spent in the two gardens before the house in London was ready for rehabilation. Holidays became important for the little chums to meet up, but in between times Joanna found it lonely without her neighbour's grandchild to play with, her dolls became her constant companions.

Pamela's notes in an address book

Started Sunday school (3yrs 4months)
Dancing classes Sept 1948
Started school Sept 20th 1949 at Priory school (Whiteleys) 4years. Got 7 stars first fortnight. Won 2nd prize first term, 1st prize 2nd term.

Patrick's diary

Jan22 1949 Dr Chase 22–24 Flue pain . . . stumoc and ears. Two weeks.
First day at school for Joanna 20 Sept 1949

Although Joanna's adoptive parents knew that she was the result of a liaison between a young married woman and an American airman and that the husband, on return from his war duties, refused to bring up the child as his own, they knew little else—as was the custom in those days. There were documents with very little detail and Joanna had no access to them, only receiving them when she reached adulthood and had completely fled the nest.

Being an only child, Joanna often daydreamed about a sister or a brother. She had been told of her adoption before she started school, and even imagined that Prince Charles might be a brother, being quite prepared to share him with Princess Anne when she was born. She showed little interest in knowing anything about her birth parents. The Hendersons had explained that they were unable to make their own baby, so they had chosen Joanna from the Church Welfare Society, making her very special. She certainly felt that she was; resulting in a zest for life which was noticeable in everything she did.

Joanna was a model pupil at school, making enormous strides, when the fees were suddenly increased. The Hendersons reluctantly transferred her to St. George's C of E school in September 1950. She suffered a bout of measles in the July. This did not spoil the summer holiday for her because a young family with a daughter had moved into the newly built Police houses near to their home. They would play in the wasteland behind the houses during the summer

days. Joanna's new friend was also going to St. George's
School, so they could travel together on the school bus.

Patrick's diary

First two double teeth out Sat 9th September 1950
Loose tooth came out 6Feb 1951
Joanna hymunised 16 July 1951
Joanna had tonsals removed 1952 April 29th. came home May1st

Joanna knew she was fortunate to live in Stamford for it was
a beautiful old market town on the edge of the fens. On fine
Sunday afternoons, the family walked to the other side of the
town and into Burghley Park. The Elizabethan house had
been built for Elizabeth 1's Chief Minister, William Cecil, the
first Lord Burghley and was extremely grand. It was now
the home of The Marquess of Exeter, who had owned the
houses on The Burghley Estate—one of which had been the
home of Patrick's parents. When Patrick had been young, he
had kept a goat that was admired by The Marquess when he
visited one day. Patrick had been finding it difficult to look
after:

"I offered it to the gentleman for a fee and to my amazement
he agreed to the price, on condition I took it up to Burghley
House. I was very pleased . . . and a bit better off."

This became folklore within the family and Patrick could
be heard regaling the story to anyone who had not heard it
before.

Sometimes there was a cricket match played on a Sunday
afternoon, which was a treat for the family, as both parents
loved the game. Patrick had played behind the stumps for his
works' team and Joanna soon learned the rules of the game
from these two enthusiasts.

Stamford's old houses and Bath House were a constant joy to
the family and they often took the long way home from town
in order to appreciate the view offered over The Meadows.
The seven splendid spires of the old churches always seemed
to shine, even when the day was cloudy and the sun was
hiding. The Meadows offered a source of freedom and fishing

opportunities for growing girls who were accompanied by their fathers on their quest for minnows from the River Welland. One such excursion was greeted with howls of laughter from Joanna's friend when her fishing net became entangled in a bramble and resulted in Joanna's departure into the briny! The girls made a bedraggled sight as they made their way through the streets of respectable Stamford. Joanna was relieved to be safely restored to her parents, along with the two minnows that were swimming in a jar of river water until they could be returned to their natural habitat.

Joanna continued to do well at school and was awarded a prize at the end of every year in Primary school. She went to St. George's Sunday School each week and thrilled at the stories she heard from a charismatic young teacher, who gave her an interest in religion.
There was daily contact with the maternal grandmother and weekly contact with Patrick's parents, so Joanna knew her grandparents well. She often saw her two cousins (Patrick's sister's boys) at the home of her grandparents on a Friday evening when the children were treated to a 'sixpenny bag', full of goodies that grandma had collected from the corner shop. Joanna felt very loved and cherished by her family.

Christmas time was very exciting as the extended family was always involved and Joanna was spoilt by doting relatives. The fifties brought with it more affluence and the family were able to spend more freely on little luxuries.

When the weather was bright, Joanna and her father could be found in the garden. Joanna had no way of remembering the time she spent in the garden with her birth mother. Like Amy, Patrick grew his own vegetables whilst Joanna dug the ground for pottery treasures. A friend of Pamela's aunt was the mother of an archaeologist so the family took an interest in the subject. Patrick and Joanna would scrub and scrutinise the pieces that had been raised from the ground once all the gardening had been completed.

Chickens were kept in the coup at the bottom of the garden. They supplied the family with eggs and meals.

"This is Bella," announced Joanna's father, as he started to carve the chicken in front of him. Joanna looked at her mother.

"Not our Bella, is it?" she asked, with tears in her eyes.

Before Pamela could reply, Patrick smiled and said,

"Of course. We keep the fowl to feed us."

"You wouldn't want to be hungry would you?" asked Pamela of her appalled daughter.

"Suppose not. But . . ."

Joanna understood the words. When she and her father fed them the next day she warned the chickens that they would be "on the table" when they stopped laying eggs. Patrick was amused, but relieved that his precious girl could 'sort things out in her mind', as he confided to Pamela later.

Joanna had problems 'learning by heart' and many hours and tears were spent on learning The Prayer of Thanksgiving for school. Tables did not give Joanna the same heartache; perhaps because there was a rhythm to them—and she loved dancing and singing.

She was tidy by nature and kept her bedroom in good order; books had a place on the bookcase that Patrick had made for her; clothes hung in a wardrobe in neat rows. Her bedside table housed a clock, the book that she was reading, a torch (until Pamela caught her reading under the covers instead of sleeping!) and a pen and paper for writing notes.
Joanna had hoped that she would be able to read when and how she wanted, but Pamela insisted that there was a time and place for everything and that jobs had to be done in the house when it was necessary.

Pamela had asked her spinster cousin to be a godmother to Joanna. Joan was delighted to carry out the duties expected of her. Her father was a Chemist and had his own business in Stamford and had married one of the beautiful Johnson girls of Warwickshire. Eliza, Joan's mother, was the youngest of the three and Emma Louise, Pamela's mother, was the eldest. The middle girl was unmarried and had looked after ailing relatives rather than pursuing a career.

Joan adored Joanna and treated her as her own, showering love and affection on her as often as possible. Joan had spent every Thursday evening with her cousin and her husband since she had returned from London. During the blitz she had lost her fiancé, Ted, who had been on Police duty. Thursday evenings meant fish and chips out of paper, something that her father would never allow, so Joan had a special place in her heart for The Hendersons.

On her visits to Joan's house, Joanna was taught how to mend and bake cakes.

"Use the weight of two eggs for the amount of flour and sugar you need to make your cake," advised Joan, "And you'll rarely make a mistake."

The Coronation of Queen Elizabeth 11 encouraged the Hendersons to buy a television set. It was a small Cosser with a screen size of 14". There were two television sets in the road; those who lived below number 24 went to number 2, and those above joined the Hendersons at number 57. Neighbours and family gathered in their front room for the historic event.

"Isn't she brave!" exclaimed Joanna's grandmother as Queen Juliana of The Netherlands rode in an open top carriage despite the pouring rain, so that everyone could see her.

"I expect she wants people to remember her," answered Patrick scathingly.

Joanna thought she was silly to get wet. Her mother was always insistent that she kept on her raincoat or sheltered under an umbrella.

"Grown-ups!" she thought.

But, it was a spectacular day and full of memories. Everyone had brought their own sandwiches, Pamela only had to supply cups of tea for the viewers.

The television became a focal point in the household. Stalin's death was reported on the News, as was the marriage of Grace Kelly to Prince Ranier of Monocco in 1956. Elvis Presley's appearance on The Ed Sullivan Show hit the headlines, which gave Patrick an opportunity to vaunt his scathing opinion of the Rock and Roll star.

Once sport began to be televised, cricket and football were constant companions of The Henderson family. In later years, Pamela gained a weakness for wrestling and boxing matches, but Joanna felt they were meaningless opportunities for men to thrash out at other men. She saw little point in watching them, being relieved that homework was too pressing for her to waste time!

By the age of eight, Joanna was a ballet and tap dancer at Mrs. Edward's School of Dancing, appearing in Stamford's annual Christmas Pantomime. She had natural talent and her parents fostered this with enthusiasm.

Realising that there had to be some grounding (Patrick was suspicious of 'acting' or any of its close relations) and that Joanna possessed a sense of rhythm, Mrs. Hatton was approached in the hope that she might provide piano lessons. Daily practice did not appeal to Joanna, but she was encouraged to do half an hour before school each day. All went well for a couple of years, until the neighbour (who had forewarned the Hendersons of trouble) complained that she was being disturbed. Pamela went into dispute as Joanna never sat down at the piano until 8o'clock, before she set off to school.

Whilst solicitors' letters winged their way through letter-boxes on Drift Road, Pamela made the mistake of scooting along the pavement between the house and that of her neighbour. This led to a visit from the local Police as the neighbour had reported Pamela 'for riding on the pavement', thus committing an offence. She was given a warning, but this led to a 'Neighbours from hell' situation with further solicitors' letters landing on the neighbours' doormats. Although Joanna was fairly oblivious, Pamela grew restless and unhappy, so it was decided that The Hendersons should move from The Drift.

They would look for another house nearer town, which was on the flat and would suit them as they got older. At this point, Joanna realised that her life would change. She would be forced to leave her friend of six years who lived only three houses away.

The girls had enjoyed true friendship. They were the members of The Secret Two, clothed in wartime blackout cloaks and Woolworth masks, a la Lone Ranger, exploring the humps and hollows in the fields behind the houses. Not only had they enjoyed the thrills of fishing, but they had played 'Cowboys and Indians' with school-friends on the land behind the house, which Patrick had bought as an investment until he found a use for it. They had shared secrets, dressed and undressed dolls, petted the animals, chatted, laughed, cried, played two-bally against the walls outside the houses, travelled to school together and been 'best friends'. Their lives outside school and hobbies revolved around each other.
What they failed to realise was that their lives were changing anyway.
Shopping, High school and the intrigues of the opposite sex were on the horizon.

Meanwhile, Joanna's parents found their television a blessing. Neither of them were Cinema lovers, or 'pub goers' as were the parents of her friend, so they chose their television programmes to fill the evenings. They were avid followers of 'What's my line?' 'Dixon of Dock Green', 'The Black and White Minstrel Show', 'Billy Cotton's Band Show', The Toppers (who brought a smile to Patrick's face as they kicked their long legs in complicated routines), 'The Sky at Night', 'Blue Peter', 'Grandstand', 'Coronation Street' and 'Z Cars'.

Pamela and Patrick were older than many parents of young children and their views and values were reflected in Joanna's rearing. It was only in later life that she realised she had been unaware of rows they might have had, or knowledge that they possessed, which would have been so useful to her had they shared it. After she was married she discovered that Patrick had been a star at Geography at school, but he had never imparted any of his knowledge or enthusiasm to her.

Her father finished work at 5pm on Fridays and Mondays rather than working overtime at the factory and Joanna's mother always made a bacon and egg fry-up for his return from work. On Fridays Pamela collected Joanna from school and they bought three cakes at the bakers on St. Paul's Street. Joanna usually chose a merinque and Pamela varied the cakes for herself and her husband each week. Patrick insisted that each cake be cut into three exact portions so that they 'could have a taste of each one'. It was a ritual that Joanna remembered with affection for all of her life and often adopted the tactic in her dealings with others.

She realised that she was very fortunate to have such loving parents and felt enormous empathy for fellow pupils were not as fortunate as herself.

One cold winter's day, Joanna looked across the playground and saw Dorothy in a thin dress and a patched coat. She herself was wrapped up in a thick winter coat, which had matching hat and gloves, so she felt snug, especially as the coat was over her favourite blue pinafore dress and red jumper. She began to think about Dorothy's predicament. Here was a child from a large family whose father drank most of his earnings before her mother had a chance to buy food for the table. Joanna's mother had been known to take round a basket of goodies, but told Joanna that she could not do it very often for fear of offending Dorothy's mother. When Joanna got home that evening, having been in trouble for not concentrating to Mrs. Granger in class, she said,

"I'm ever so worried about Dorothy."

"Why is that?" asked Pamela, noticing the concern in her daughter's voice.

"She doesn't seem to have any warm clothes."

"Oh dear. I wonder if we can find something that isn't too obviously new for her," replied Pamela.

"What about that Fair Isle beret I had last year? I can manage with the one that matches my coat," suggested Joanna, who had already given some thought as to what she would be allowed to surrender to someone else.

Pamela pondered for a moment. It was how she had hoped Joanna would react to problems and people who were not as fortunate as herself.

"If you're sure, darling."

"Oh yes."

"Do you know where it is?"

"It's in the cupboard under the stairs I think."

"Ok. You go and look for it while I make us a pot of tea," said a proud Pamela, who had noticed that her young daughter was becoming thoughtful of others.

Dorothy was thrilled with the woollen beret and it warmed Joanna's heart to see her in it in the playground the day after she had given it to her.

Years later, Joanna saw Dorothy's wedding photograph in the top Stamford photographer's window. It was a regal affair and when she asked her mother about it, she learned that Dorothy had become a nurse, fallen in love with a doctor and subsequently married him.

"What a wonderful fairy tale ending for her," said Joanna when she heard the news.

"Yes, isn't it? And Dorothy's mother is thriving since her feckless husband died about two months after Dorothy's wedding. She's beginning to realise what life is really about poor dear. She goes to a meeting every week that Aunty Fay attends for widows and they have become quite friendly, which is nice for them both."

In February 1955, nine—and—a—half year old Joanna and her friend, who was almost a year older than her, sat the eleven plus examination. Pupils who passed were given the opportunity to attend the Direct Grant Schools in the town; an opportunity not to be ignored. Joanna found the papers in the examination reasonably easy and did not give the outcome another thought.

One day in May, a letter arrived from the Education Authority, telling the Hendersons that their daughter had passed the first stage of the selection process and had an appointment with the Headmistress of Stamford High School for Girls on the following Wednesday. There was a form to complete and return to the Headmistress, which was duly done and Pamela and Patrick spent a couple of sleepless nights before Joanna's interview.

Joanna sat at the desk in a small room "within these walls of grey" with a dozen other young girls and wrote a composition, answered a comprehension paper and completed an Arithmetic paper. She then had an interview with the Headmistress in which she remembered to smile and reported that she had felt at ease with the attractive woman on the other side of a rather large desk. Her friend also had a similar experience and both families were delighted when the girls were offered places at the prestigious school. Only five pupils from their school had passed and there would be only a handful of 'Scholarship girls' in the year. A splendid uniform, new shoes, P.E. kit and labels were purchased from Parishes and the girls were told to talk of nothing else but their future lives with privileged girls. Neither of them realised how fortunate they were to have been selected to attend these establishments.

"Don't waste the opportunities," warned her godmother, "only a few girls get this chance. The world is your oyster."

Patrick's diary

Started high school 20 Sept 1955. Upper III class. Only just 10 in July!
Her friend is in Upper111R. Prob a good thing. They can make new friends.
The house has been sold. We shall move in early December, so it will be different for the girls anyway.

Joanna was devastated to be in a different class from her friend. The school was huge and she felt overwhelmed by all the corridors, teachers in gowns and books. She could not bear to be parted from Angela. The same conversations were being had at the Police house up the road. The girls' mothers met and reassured their daughters that nothing need change, even after The Hendersons had moved, because they could bike to each other's house and still see each other. So, life would still be good.

By this time Joanna had stopped biting her nails and with the encouragement of her Great Aunt Liz had pushed back cuticles and shaped her nails into respectability.

"Now aren't they lovely, my darling," she said when she inspected them on one of the family's visits for tea.

Joanna purred with pleasure whilst her mother smiled conspiratorially with her Aunt. It gave her an incentive to keep her nails clean and well-shaped. All girls going out into the world need to be well-groomed and respectable as she knew from the people who mattered to her: her mother, father, grandmothers, godmother and great uncle and aunt.

She also knew that she would be able to watch decent dramas on the television, under the guise of 'bettering herself' and 'being like the other girls in my class'.

Once Joanna had started the High School, Pamela became a 'dinner-lady' at a small primary school. Sometimes Joanna was on holiday when this school was still working, so she was able to heat up the meal for her father when he came in for his lunch. She enjoyed playing at keeping house and relished the opportunity to wash up the pots and clean the surfaces.

Joanna's relationship with her mother was very close and she told her everything that had happened during the day. Pamela was delighted to be included in Joanna's life and often pitied the poor woman who had been forced to surrender her small baby in 1945.

Chapter 11   A Move To The West Country

As she was only just over a year old when her mother became pregnant for a second time, Norma could not have realised the dilemma that must have confronted Amy Jackson. She remembers her mother making a birthday cake and as she liked sultanas, she shared them with her baby sister. She thought she was being kind, but her mother had a different slant on the situation and seemed quite cross at the time.

After William's return from the war, life gradually got back to normal and Amy and William tried to make the most of their life together.
They both knew that their family life was important and William tried hard to be a good father to Norma, although he found it difficult to relax or be playful. Amy thought it may be because he had the horrors of war embossed on his brain, but when she asked questions of him, William blanked her and refused to give her any details—just said,

"Oh you don't want to know what it was like. I was lucky; I came home. Some didn't."

Her mother assured her that he would eventually open up, but this was not the case and he never shared his wartime experiences with her.
Amy felt bewildered and shut out from her husband. She tried to laugh off her doubts, forget her wonderful love affair with Guy and concentrate on loving her little girl and rebuilding her shattered marriage to William. As often as possible she found time to visit her parents so that she could unburden her heavy heart to her mother.
Joanna was not mentioned in William's presence, but Amy had to tell someone of her heartache and her mother was the one who seemed to understand her predicament.

"Don't worry too much, my love", she reassured her daughter. "You know she is with nice people and will be looked after. It was the only thing you could have done."

The same words every time we speak, thought Amy, but it doesn't make things any easier. She was tempted to start her diary writing again, but feared that William would react badly if he found it, so decided that for the moment she had better stick to confiding in her mother.

Norma soon stopped asking about her sister and played happily with her friends on the base. She enjoyed digging in the garden, filling a small watering can with water and pouring it out over the seeds that her mother had planted with her in the triangle between the grass and the vegetables.

"One day your vegetables will have grown so much that we shall be able to eat them for our dinner," she told her child.

"Oh. That'll be good," Norma responded enthusiastically.

Amy still baked each Thursday in preparation for the weekend. She worked especially hard for Sunday, when William usually managed a few hours at home with them after church.

As her mother baked, Norma stood on the small kitchen stool at her side and watched the ingredients become something mouth watering after the cooking. One of the best moments in this activity was when her mother had put all the mixture into the cake tin and handed the bowl and spoon to Norma to lick. The taste was unexplainable—just heavenly. The texture in her mouth made Norma shiver with delight and she was almost heartbroken when the bowl was clean.

Eventually she asked, "Could I make my own cake, Mummy?"

"Of course. Next time, we'll make one together."

This was the start of Norma's ability to produce delicious meals and cakes. Later, she had need of these skills in order to keep her father fed.

When he first came home Norma did not feel at ease with her father who had been absent for so much of her young life. War had traumatized him. He had lost any sparkle that had drawn Amy to him all those years ago. He had also lost the ability to converse with the world or his needy family.

When Norma was five, she started school on the base and proved to be an able pupil who would go far.

Amy had been excited to find herself pregnant again in 1950, but the little boy was still-born so she once again swallowed her heartbreak and put all her efforts into making life for their small family as normal as possible.

But life was difficult.

William was free with his smacking and Norma and her mother were often on the receiving end of his wrath. Despite having a good job, there seemed to be little money for extras and Norma was unable to attend additional classes to those she had in school. She loved music and dance just as much as her mother, but never had the opportunity to foster these inborn traits. They swirled around the living room when William was not in sight. He had lost his love for music and dance which had played such an important role in meeting his wife. Had he been asked, he would have insisted that he liked music and loved his wife and daughter dearly, but he was not demonstrative with his feelings and both Amy and Norma felt they had to rely on each other for any physical display of affection.

William continued to claim his nuptial rights and Amy tried to remain a loving and giving wife to him. But their relationship had been damaged. By the time their baby boy had been still born and she had had three miscarriages, she began to feel that perhaps she was being punished for Guy and Joanna. She had long discussions with the vicar and the welfare officer on the base and both were understanding and eager to listen, but it did not ease the burden that she carried.

Norma's fair auburn hair, green gold eyes and ready smile gave her a dazzling appearance and she was a popular friend in school with both boys and girls. She had some tomboy ways but her mother kept her in check and knew that by teaching her to cook and clean she would eventually become a good housewife. No one expected her to follow in her mother's footsteps, service was dying out as modern appliances came onto the market and people found that these were cheaper than employing servants. Amy wanted her daughter to be a worthy catch for a suitable young man when she was old enough.

They went to the cinema occasionally—when William was not too tired or irritable, or when Amy nagged him enough.

Norma was content to play with the games that her parents and grandparents bought for her as Christmas and birthday presents. Her parents bought her a rabbit for Christmas when she was six, but she had asked for a cat. Eventually, after much whining and sulking, William promised her the cat for her birthday if he could find one. He did. Norma showered love onto 'Bertie' and petted him as often as she could, cuddling into his soft, grey fur and telling him all her troubles and frustrations, of which there were many.

She occasionally saw her maternal grandparents, but usually when there had been a crisis. Sometimes her grandmother visited on her own which was a great treat, because Norma received more attention. There was little money for trips away from the base, so relations had to visit The Jacksons. Amy's cousin, Albert came when he 'was in the area', which Norma could not fully understand. After his visits, her father was usually irritable and there were often shouting episodes between her parents—she secretly wondered in later years if Albert (not William) was her father, but nothing was ever said about this possibility.

Norma enjoyed climbing the trees with her friends on the base and they often made dens and ran around in knickers and no tops when it was hot—and sometimes when it was only warm, when sensible people would be wearing cardigans over jumpers! The summers always seemed to herald good weather when Norma was young, so happiness reigned for her.

Tragedy struck in 1951.

Norma was only seven years old when her mother started to fall in and around the home. This frightened everybody.

Amy resumed her diary writing in the hope that she could vent her anxieties and thoughts to someone who would not judge her.

Amy's diary 1951

February 4th.
Oh God, whatever is happening? When I look in the mirror my eyes seem to be hooded and my mouth droops. Have I had a stroke or something? Is this God's way of punishing me for the baby? I try not to think of her, but when I do it is like an arrow through my heart. I don't seem to be able to keep my balance any more. Bill seems to be worried thank goodness, but the doctors don't seem to know what it is. Have even had some tests at the hospital, but this just leads to further tests and no one says much except telling me not to worry. A fat chance that is! I can't even pick up a basket of washing without feeling that I'm going to drop it again. I am so tired all the time and this silly eye keeps twitching and blurring.

April 8th
Still no reason for this stupid shake or giddiness. I am always wanting to pee and sometimes can't make the toilet—very awkward when we go out—not that we go far or even often. The old legs feel numb sometimes and my left foot won't go where I want it to.
Poor Norma is having to help out a bit. She isn't 8 until September, but she's very good in the house and I don't know what I'd do without her. I only have to tell her once and a meal is waiting for her dad when he comes home. Not sure he realises quite what she is doing to keep the house together.
I wonder if this is why I couldn't carry another child? Or is it my punishment??

The problem was eventually diagnosed (three days after Norma's eighth birthday) as Multiple Sclerosis, a disease that little was known about at that time, except that it often hit women in their 30s and could progress quickly. It was a distressing time and Amy was not sure if she was relieved to know that she had this unpredictable problem.

May was as helpful as she had always been, but many of the household chores then became part of Norma's life. William made few allowances and expected Norma to be able to run a home as efficiently as her mother.

Suddenly, Amy's mother, Alice, became ill. Amy's body refused to let her go to her and care for her, and it was with great sadness that she learned about her mother's death via a telegram only a week after the one that had brought news of the illness. Amy felt shattered; Alice had been Amy's backbone and confidant. Although May was a wonderful neighbour, nothing could replace the love and support of a mother.

Amy was thankful that she had taught her small child the rudimentaries of keeping house, for this burden fell on the young, tender shoulders of her tiny 'woman'. Tears of frustration and unease poured down her face many times a day. Tablets did little to ease the pain and no words of comfort could mend her heart. She began to pray and found her comfort in prayer and The Bible. Music was important to her, but she could no longer dance around the room or swing her daughter under her arm as Guy had once swung her. Life had to be more static, although she managed to keep the garden under control as long as Norma was there to aid her in getting up and down.

Everything comes at once—it's a well-known fact.

William's expertise was needed at the new Radio Station at RAF Gowley. Amy would be sad to leave her friend behind, but May and her husband were also expecting to move away from the base as he was about to retire from the forces.

The South West of England was a long way from her original roots and her father. Amy felt very hesitant and anxious. Norma felt resentful that she had to accompany her parents to Somerset and leave her circle of friends behind in East Anglia.

"You'll be able to have them to stay," said William dismissively, but Norma knew that life was about to change irrevocably for her.
Initially she was very lonely. She had been deeply hurt to find her young life turned upside down, having been forced to leave friends that she had made in school.

The first few months after they had moved, were a nightmare for Norma. William was caught up in his new post and Amy seemed to tire easily, only able to walk a few steps at a time. She was becoming reliant on walking aids and help from her daughter.

Norma's grandfather was miles away in East Anglia. He had been devastated that his daughter and family were to move so far away from him so soon after losing his beloved wife. William had reassured him by saying that he would enjoy a week at the sea-side every year and that he could keep in touch by letter each week, which was quite ironic considering that Alice had always done the writing of any letters.

Secretly, William was pleased that his wife and daughter would be parted from his father-in-law. Both he and his wife had been supportive of their daughter over her adultery and the subsequent birth of the bastard who had ruined their lives. Try as he may, William could not forget what had happened whilst he was abroad "fighting for King and country". Nobody provided counselling for such men and they were expected to continue as though nothing had happened. He found life very tough; memories of the war and the deceit of his lovely wife had made him feel bitter. Now, she had become ill.

Looking after a new house, which smelt of illness and was always deathly quiet; caring for a sick mother *and* making new friends at school kept Norma awake at night. She had no old friends to talk to about her situation and she was worried that people would make fun of her and her mother, who seemed to be struggling more every day.

But living had to go on and The Jacksons gradually settled into a routine on the base near Weston-Super-Mare. At the weekends when William was free, they sometimes made trips into the seaside town where Norma played on the sands and in the water when the tide allowed.

Being a gregarious child, despite her initial worries, she soon made new friends at school, but she rarely felt happy. Her father continued to be too free with his slaps, both to his wife and his daughter, which was heartbreaking for Amy.

She knew that she probably deserved all the punishment he administered, although he was quite irrational in his admonishment, but her young daughter was guilty of nothing but caring love.

Norma helped her father cultivate the garden. Amy realised that he was eventually trying to keep some form of order in the household and hoped that the move away from East Anglia was helping him to heal.

Growing vegetables gave a sense of calmness to Norma. Her mother often watched and gave her advice.

"I may not be able to do much," she said, "but I can tell you what's needed to be done!"

In between gardening and cooking, Norma found time to be with her friends. Strong bonds were formed between the girls as they grew up alongside each other. She told her 'best friend', Catherine, about the problems at home, although did not confide too much. She was reluctant to let her know that her father had a violent temper, which sometimes erupted like a volcano, leaving she and her mother speechless and hurt. Some things had to be borne alone and with dignity. They were allowed to impose on sleep and comfort, but should not be aired in public; they were too shameful to be in the wide world, outside the confines of her home. She must bear the pain and troubles of family life and try to make life as bearable as possible for her suffering mother. She prayed every night in the firm belief that God would help her. When it was possible, she and her parents went to the local church, but it was always an effort for Amy to get ready and walk the few streets necessary.

Fortunately, Norma was intelligent and passed the eleven plus at the age of ten, which meant that she could attend the local Grammar School and make the world her oyster, but Norma felt restless and frightened. No one else in her group had passed the examinations and she did not want to become isolated. She remembered how unhappy she had felt when she had been uprooted from security in East Anglia and was determined not to become trapped in that sense of despair again.

If it had not been for her precious cat and rabbit, she felt that she would have died from despondency.

Norma's diary

March 1953
Hate school. Don't want to go to Grammar school and do Latin: what's the point of that? All my friends are going to Statham Comp. It has a swimming pool and is NEW. Will have to persuade ma and pa that I needn't go. Sometimes I miss gran and gramps; they didn't come over much but they always seemed to know what to do for the best.

April 1953.
Awful row with ma about school. The old man started when he got home. Will have to keep on about it. I AM NOT GOING TO THAT STUPID SCHOOL. Phoned Catherine and told her I shall make a stand. I want to be with her and the others.

By this time, Amy was too poorly to take any responsibility for decision-making and William found the strain of a bright, energetic daughter and a sick wife too demanding to be rational, so Norma was able to decide that Grammar School, where they 'did' Latin, was not for her.
The newly built Comprehensive School in the nearby village was more attractive to her and her friends, so instead of taking advantage of the opportunities offered to anyone who passed the 11+, Norma went along to the Comprehensive School.

She sailed through the lessons and as she was never stretched, did a limited amount of work and soon became disillusioned. The teachers moaned occasionally and her reports were a disappointment to her parents. She knew how far to stretch the Staff's patience—after all, she had a father who beat her for less reason than she gave to her teachers at school. She never did anything too outrageous which could lead to a suspension. She loved swimming and spent many hours after school swimming up and down the pool with her friends before returning home and being confronted with jobs or sadness.

Her parents were so involved with their own problems that they allowed Norma freedom to come and go as she pleased as long as she cooked the necessary meals, baked the necessary cakes for the week and cleaned the house. Money remained short so she was forced to make her own entertainment and she and her friends often went into Weston-super-Mare at the weekends and continued to enjoy the beach and the facilities offered by the seaside town. They were all such competent swimmers, none of the parents worried about their off spring, and the tide only came in twice a day before going out a long way, so it was quite a safe place for youngsters to enjoy themselves.

Norma was happy when she had been with friends, it eased the atmosphere at home and provided respite from the disagreements and disharmony between daughter and parents.

She loved going to the cinema. She adored Marlon Brando, Cary Grant, (who was a Bristolian), James Dean and Laurence Olivier. Her favourite film was 'Gentlemen Prefer Blondes'. Marilyn Monroe singing 'Diamonds are a girl's best friend' was her idea of what life should be like. She was determined to become a blond one day and own rings and necklaces of diamonds. This would mean a good marriage and a wealthy life-style (perhaps in America . . .). How many romantics was the cinema responsible for?

Norma and her friends sometimes went into Bristol on the train. These excursions were fun and often very interesting. When her friends were busy with their own family life, Norma would catch the train alone just to look around the shops and see the latest fashions that she read about in her weekly magazine. She loved to listen in to other people's conversations, especially when she only had her magazine for company.

On one occasion she recalled over-hearing:

". . . a wonderful pattern. Turquoises, blues, pinks. Very complicated," said a lady on one side of the carriage.

"My staff would get excited with some of these ideas. I can see one of them . . ."from a gentleman in a business suit on the other side.

"Of course, she wanted something different from her sister." said the lady to her companion.

"If you could put it on paper . . ."encouraged the business man.

She returned to her magazine, but found she was distracted again.
A rasping, grating voice was saying:

"He jumped off the mountain and his femur ended up through his brain."

"At least he won't have known much about it," replied the companion.

The things people talk about, thought Norma.

"My imagination began to work overtime and I was relieved to draw into a village station where several of them got off," she told Catherine as she shared her experience later.

She had gathered up her errant thoughts and returned to the Woman's Own she had purchased from the paper stall at Weston Station. Once again she was enticed into listening:

"No. From the helicopter."

"Oh, yes."

Now, what was that conversation about? Perhaps she could use these snippets of conversation at school. Perhaps it was about someone from the base. Wonder if it was anyone she knew?

She thought about her father and his recent promotion. That should keep the parents busy and stop them discussing her when they thought she wasn't listening.

Chapter 12   Someone To Care

Swimming and train journeys rarely lead to trouble, but friendship and hormones are another matter, particularly if unhappiness and unfulfilment dominate. Bertie was a great help to her, but he was never able to give her an answer to her problems and Norma began to find that she needed to unburden herself to someone other than her beloved cat.

Norma's diary

May 1957
Gorgeous Greek boy new to the school. Parents bought the hotel in town. Perhaps they're rich!? His sister is in Catherine's class. She said he is going to be put in my set for Maths so I can get to know him there!
Later : he is older than us, so won't be taught with us. Expect he won't have much to do with us. Shall have to work on his sister!

Norma and her friends did enough work to keep out of trouble with the Headmaster, but her teachers were aware that she was under-performing in every subject except Gym and Games. In these areas she was able to use up all her pent up energies and anxieties. She was able to be Norma Jackson, instead of the daughter of an abusive father and a mother who needed to be cared for.

She dreamed of being loved—especially by Alexis—and craved to be special and the centre of someone's world. Norma and her friends became detached from their parents and like true teenagers, immersed themselves in music, gossip and each other. They were fascinated by the new sound of Rock n Roll and Norma was hooked on Elvis Presley.

William was beginning to earn a good wage. Norma begged her mother to talk to her father about buying her a Dansette Record Player so that she could listen to records along with her friends.

"She's a good girl, Bill. Does SO much in the house. I couldn't manage without her."

"Yes, I know. But a record player is a bit rash."

"But she deserves a treat. Just think of all the meals and cakes she cooks, and the cleaning she does. Not to mention the garden."

"I'll think about it."

It was a start.

Norma was on her best behaviour for a week after her mother told her how the conversation had gone. Eventually, William agreed that she could have the record player for her birthday. Until then, the girls had to rely on hearing Elvis on Radio Luxembourg 208 or on headphones in the large Record Departments in Bristol.

Boys were another favourite topic in their conversations. Norma watched Alexis, talked to his sister and prayed that he would notice her.

Norma's Diary

July 1958
At last. Alexis has asked me out. We went to the cinema to see 'Indiscreet' starring CARY GRANT & Ingrid Bergman—not bad, and then to the beach. UMM!

At the age of fifteen, she found herself completely involved with the Greek boy and was going on frequent dates with him. Norma loved the excitement that she felt with Alexis. He only had to appear and she felt herself surrendering to his presence. It was inevitable that their dates would lead to a more amorous relationship. The place did not concern them when their passion overwhelmed them. They usually walked along the beach and the prom, with their arms around each other, eating candy floss or ice creams purchased from the stalls on The Pier. Towards the end of the evening, Norma and Alexis would find themselves under the pier or in a secluded alley. He would press his lips to hers and she melted. Gradually the kisses led to light petting, but Norma did not temper his embraces.

Alexis was 17 in May 1959 and his parents bought him a van. By this time, Norma was head over heels in love with him and their union in the back of his van was breathtaking beyond her expectations—and private to the prying eyes of the outside world.

They dated regularly. Norma was completely bewitched by her lover and took enormous risks to be with him. School took second place to their meetings. Her parents seemed to be oblivious to her wanton ways and were alerted to her non-attendance at school only when the Welfare Officer called.

William beat her on her return 'from school', Amy sobbed and Norma fought back tears. She became more determined to ignore her parents, school and authority. Alexis made her happy.

Because her mother was too incapacitated to parent her with any force and her father was often on duty at the base, she still managed to go out in the evenings. Each night with Alexis ended in passionate love making in his van and, inevitably, this resulted in a pregnancy.

Even Buddy Holly's premature death in 1959 evaded Norma's thoughts, although she had enjoyed his music. Alexis was her reason for existence and her obsession with him had no bounds.

Norma's diary.

March 1960
Oh, God, no curse again. Alexis says I'll have to tell mum and dad. HELP! Imagine their reaction . . . At least he says he'll stick by me—whatever that means.

Norma knew that she should confess her predicament to her parents.

"I expect it's that Greek lad you're always with. Don't think I haven't heard about you," spat her father.

"You've never said anything, Bill," said Amy.

"You've enough to worry about. You'd think she'd have thought about all our problems."

He lifted his arm. His face like thunder.

"Don't hurt her Bill," screamed Amy.

"Oh. I expect you'll understand. Like mother, like daughter," her husband shouted, now beside himself with rage.

Norma looked disbelievingly at her father. What was he implying?

"The best thing you can do, my girl," he snarled, "is pack your bags and go and live with *his* lot . . . They've enough rooms in that hotel, so you won't starve."

Norma began to plead with him.

"Please don't send me away. Surely I can stay here and have the baby?"

"You surely can't. What will people say? Girls like you and your mother should go away to one of those Mother & Baby Homes that cater for types like you."

"What does he mean Mum?" asked Norma, turning to her mother, whose head had dropped into her chest.

"Go on. Tell her, you bitch. I'm going to the pub."

He turned to his daughter, whose face was crumpled with sadness and bewilderment.

"Make sure you're gone by tomorrow night. There's no place for you in this house."

William stormed out.

Amy put her arms out to her sobbing daughter and drew her towards the sofa next to her. They were both shaking with fear and distress.

"That's typical of the way your father works," Amy said, trying to control her own thoughts.

"But why did he say, "Like mother, like daughter?"

Amy took a deep breath. She realised that she would now have to talk about her adultery during the War and her lost child. Although she thought of her daily, she no longer mentioned Joanna. Guy was now a memory. This made him even more precious and Amy vowed that she would not tell Norma too much about the man she had truly loved.

"You had a sister when Dad was away in India. She wasn't his child and when he came back from the war, he insisted that I gave her up."

Norma was shaken by this news. At first she did not know how to react, but she asked her mother,

"How could you let her go?"

"Well, you needed your father and I still loved him in a way."

"But . . . it was your baby."

"There were lots of war babies and some on the base. It wasn't unusual for mothers to let their little ones go in the circumstances."

"How old was she?"

"Nearly three months."

"Did I know her?"

"Oh, yes. You loved her dearly."

"What did I do with her?"

"You kissed her, rocked her; oh, and one day when I was making a cake, you fed her with sultanas—until I realised!"

"Were you cross with me?"

"I expect I shouted. I know I was relieved that I could get them out of her mouth."

"Do you know where she went to?"

"I did at the time, but I've blanked it out so it doesn't hurt any more."

Norma thought about this latest piece of information.

"Goodness. I've got a sister. Do you know, I think I remember an incident with sultanas. Because I liked them so much, I thought she would?!"

"Yes," laughed Amy.

Norma looked at her mother.

Talking about her lost child seemed to have restored a sparkle. Something that had been missing for many years. No doubt her miscarriages and her still—born son had left their scars. Norma was full of compassion. She began to draw her mother towards her, intending to embrace her, but she was stopped by Amy saying,

"But at the moment we've got more important things to worry about. I'll support you as much as I can. We'll find you somewhere to live nearby . . . I'll never stop loving you, so try not to worry too much."

Norma wondered how her mother had been able to bear the heartbreak of losing so many attempts at motherhood. She decided that she must be stronger mentally than she was physically. Everyone commented that she was so slight that she looked as though a puff of wind would blow her away.

As William had refused to stand by his daughter, Alexis' parents stepped into the breach and offered Norma a room at the hotel they ran on the sea front. In return, Norma was expected to run errands and help generally around the hotel. As Norma got closer to the birth of her baby life became more difficult, she was *still* expected to carry heavy cases and crates.

Norma met her mother regularly and on one occasion, when tiredness had made her tearful, she admitted that the situation at the hotel was not ideal. Amy was suddenly alerted to the problems that were facing her precious daughter. She decided to approach the Council. A flat was found for Norma.

Family pressures made life extremely difficult so that it was impossible for her and Alexis to set up home together. Realising that she might have to support herself and her child, Norma decided to embark on a short-hand typist course with a view to taking on secretarial work.

Using her creative talents inherited from her mother, Norma made curtains for her flat and prepared a home for herself and her unborn child. She also wanted Alexis to enjoy a homely atmosphere when he visited. Amy was delighted to see how her daughter responded to her predicament and had many feelings of remorse over how she had allowed William to dominate their lives. She wondered if she should have intervened more forcibly when her husband had frequently chastised their daughter. Had she been a stronger character might her family not be the alienated unit it now was?

Chapter 13   Life As A Single Mum

The baby was born in October,1960 and Norma's mother was delighted with her new born grandson. He looked like his father, with attractive olive skin and big, brown eyes which captured the hearts of those who saw him in his pram.

Norma was unable to find work. No employer would allow her to take the baby with her, so she made the most of keeping her small flat clean and tidy, cooking for herself and her new son. He was a good child and was adored by everyone.

She bought a small television on Hire Purchase and watched the news avidly (a habit that she had acquired on cinema visits) and was delighted when 'The Avengers' hit the small screen.

She was also an avid reader, although had not inherited her mother's love of poetry. As a member of the local library she was able to collect books and change them regularly; it gave her a purpose to go out into the town with her new son in his pram.

Alexis was proud of his son and, initially, visited him daily. Norma was thrilled that she could still call him her boyfriend. After all, she loved him with all her being. Alexis reveled in the role of doting father and decided he wanted to become part of a family, so he proposed to Norma, who was only too pleased to accept.

They chose a date for their marriage and prayed that they could get parental permission.

Although William did not support Norma, he realised that his wife helped her as much as she could, so he was easily persuaded to sign the necessary documents. Alexis' parents were delighted that their son and his girl would be part of their extended family and prepared the hotel for a great celebration. A wedding was much more acceptable than an illegitimate child.

Her son was almost two years old and Norma rejoiced in dressing him smartly for the big occasion. On the eagerly awaited day, Norma arrived at the Registry Office in good time, along with her parents and friends.

Alexis did not—and neither did her period . . .

She was pregnant again, with no prospect of changing her name.

At first she did not know what to do, but Alexis turned up at her door on the day after he should have become Norma's husband. He could not offer an explanation for his failure to turn up to be married—except that he felt he was not ready for such commitment. He assured her that he would continue to be a good father to his son so she agreed to let him come and go as he pleased and to share her bed whenever he needed to.

"I've something to tell you," she started one evening as they sat holding hands on the sofa.

She took a deep breath, "I'm pregnant again."

"Oh no!" was the reply.

Alexis put his head in his hands.

"My period didn't come on the day we should have been married."

"But that's three months ago."

"Yes . . . I'm three months pregnant."

There was silence for a few moments. Norma's heart was beating faster than a moth's wings. What would Alexis do?

At last, he turned to her and took her hands in his,

"Oh, well. We'll just be a bigger family," he smiled and took her in his arms.

Norma could not have felt happier. Her man was as pleased as she was frightened about another child. Making ends meet was a constant worry for Norma and Alexis contributed little to the upkeep or rearing of his children. But, Norma was prepared to forgive him anything. He was her life, apart from her beloved son, and she was able to overcome all difficulties if Alexis loved her.

Alexis continued to visit regularly and insisted on being present at the hospital when Norma gave birth to his second child.

It was a tricky confinement but eventually a beautiful little girl was born. She, like her brother, had shiny olive skin and big, brown eyes. Like everyone who saw them, Norma found them attractive children.
She lavished love on her offspring, made clothes from scraps of material she picked up from the shops and decided that she could make a proper home for her family. Alexis seemed to be delighted and showered them all with love and flowers or non useful presents. He was unable to see that financial help was more important if Norma was to have sufficient means to put food onto the table for the family. If Alexis moved in with his children and her mother, as was his suggestion, she would have to find a way to encourage him to give her housekeeping.

"I shall need to have some money each week", she said tentatively one evening when they were discussing the possibility of him moving in.

"Of course," he smiled. "I earn enough at dad's hotel, so don't worry, my little chicken."

He rarely used endearments with her (although often showered them onto the children) so Norma was almost speechless.

"Good."

"I'll move in next Thursday on my day off then," he said, as though it was a forgone conclusion.

Norma was thrilled and her excitement rubbed off on the children.

All went well for three months, but then Norma began to suspect that he was seeing someone else. Because he was so young and charming to the opposite sex, Alexis soon tired of fatherhood and began to stay away over night.
He moved out after confessing that he had been unfaithful to her. Norma had screamed that she could not bear to have him in the house any longer. She had been betrayed again, she would never have him back after this.

Once she had put her children to bed Norma spent her evenings watching the television or reading books that she fetched from the library. By 1962, 'Z Cars' was a regular feature of her week. She found she could afford a daily newspaper to help her to keep abreast of current affairs and to exercise her brain with its crosswords.

Alexis sent messages begging her to let him see his family and promising to be a better father and lover to her. There was no talk of marriage and he always made an excuse for not making Norma his wife, so she was determined to stand firm on her decision of keeping him at arms length. At first she resisted all his advances and sweet talking, but eventually she softened and convinced herself that it was good for the children if their father came round to visit them.

Although Norma knew that Alexis was unfaithful to her and was enjoying his life—she lived in a small community and her girlfriends were never reticent in spreading the latest gossip. In spite of all she heard love has its own way of behaving and she still found him bewitching.

The bell buzzed. Thank goodness, thought Norma, Mum's here. As she opened the door, she saw the kind face of her mother and burst into tears. Her mother put out her arms.

"I'm pregnant again," Norma sobbed.

Amy held her close. Oh, not AGAIN, she thought. Wonder who this one belongs to? It's obvious the other two are Alexis' offspring. He's gone, I expect she's had a fling with someone.

She led her wayward daughter through into the kitchen, patting the head of her precious grandson and glancing into the cot where Alice was taking a nap.

"Ganma, Ganma", squealed Alexis, standing up and clutching at Amy's knees.

"Hello, darling . . . That's a lovely thing you're making," she said, admiring the contraption that Alexis was constructing out of Meccano that she and William had bought him for Christmas.

"Finish it off for us while we have a cuppa, eh?"

Alexis dropped back onto his haunches and Amy gently led her daughter to the chair at the kitchen table. She put on the kettle to boil and placed the tealeaves into the brown earthenware teapot.

"Well then," she said directing her attention towards Norma. "Who?"

"Alexis of course," retorted Norma.

"But I thought you'd sent him packing."

"Yes, but he has to come back and see the kids, doesn't he?"

"I thought you were going to manage without him."

"I know I was, but it didn't seem fair on him."

"Hm. He really knows how to get to you, doesn't he?"

"I can't resist him. I mean to be strong, but then he arrives, and . . ."

Amy thought about Guy. Yes, she knew what that type of love and attraction was.

"What does he say?"

"He doesn't know yet."

"So, when did you last see him?"

"Oh, a bit ago," replied Norma evasively.

"When?" insisted her mother.

"Last month."

"I see . . . So, how many months are you?" asked Amy, looking at Norma's midriff.

"Three," replied Norma sadly.

"O.K. Well, we'll have to get somewhere bigger for you to live. It's already too small for you and two children, so it will be impossible with another."

"How am I going to feed us all?" wailed Norma.

"God'll find a way . . . We'll just have to get going on finding a place for you all."

"Alexis will be furious."

"Huh. Does he give you anything for the kids? Well, anything useful, like money?"

"Not a lot. But he does visit them sometimes."

"And how will he be about another baby?"

"Not sure."

Deep down, Norma knew that he would not care and would probably blame her for getting pregnant.

"Well, let's drink our tea and then we'll clear up and go up to The Town Hall and see if they can help."

Norma was amazed at how her mother could rise to a crisis. She was almost crippled with M.S., but at times like this she seemed to find an inner strength, which Norma could only admire.

When Alexis heard that another child was to be born to them, he panicked. To her horror, he decided to return to his homeland.

Norma was devastated. The man she loved had gone from her life forever.

When she was seven months pregnant, Norma moved in to a bigger flat in the Old Town. It had two bedrooms, so she and the baby could have one of them and Alexis and Alice could share the other. She used her curtain making skills and, with her mother's help, had created a pleasant home for the children before her third child was born.

Norma was nineteen and had three children under four. She would be unable to work until they were at school. Norma's mother convinced William that it was their duty to visit whenever it was convenient. Norma understood that Amy was not able to be autonomous, but she enjoyed sharing the development of her beautiful babies with her whenever she could. Her parents offered little monetary support and it was a difficult time. She kept her babies spotlessly clean and well groomed and her mother and friends helped her out as much as they possibly could. Taking the children out was a mammoth expedition, but she held her head high and ignored the stares. The residents of the town soon became accustomed to the fatherless family walking through the town or parks.

Alexis' parents were supportive of her and saw their grandchildren every week. Norma's friends gave her time and love, so she had frequent company in her flat during the week. She refused to go out with them. She felt her children would be damaged even more than they were going to be without a father figure, if she did not take her responsibilities seriously. Norma knew that she had to be firm with her children in order to provide security and love. Without a man it was hard work, but she could not face a relationship with anyone else but Alexis.

Once all the children were at school, Norma began to lead a more normal life. Eventually, after a number of job applications, Norma was able to find work as a secretary. She only heard of the love of her life when she met his sister. Then she learned of his continued philandering.

How she bore her problems, Norma never knew. Her children brought her much comfort and, as they all favoured their father in looks, she felt that he had not really left her.

She loved The Beatles pop group and listened to their records on her old radio, watched them on Top of the Pops and taught herself to jive. She sobbed through 'Cathy Come Home' on the television; lapped up the information and new technology on 'Tomorrow's World' and enjoyed 'Dr. Who', especially when Patrick Troughton replaced William Hartnell in 1966.

Norma made the most of her life. She fought like a tiger for her children's rights, especially at school, kept a clean house and filled empty hours of the day with cooking from meagre rations. The children never went hungry and often complimented her on a new dish that she had created. Sometimes, she even cooked special cakes for her friend's children's birthday parties. She realised that she had a lot to thank her mother for when it came to housekeeping.

Chapter 14   From Drift to Derby via Conduit

Joanna soon settled into her new house and her friend collected her each morning so that they could bike to school. Stamford High School for Girls was a Direct Grant school and had fee-paying girls. There was a Boarding House, which consisted of Welland House for the Junior department which ensured that the right 'calibre' of girl was seen at the establishment. The school took scholarship girls each year and Joanna and her friend, Angela, were two of them. They were not in the same form but went to and from school together. They soon made other friends—in fact, Joanna was such a sweet young girl that she became somewhat of a "pet" in the class. Before long she was enjoying trips to other girls' houses, many of whom came from a different social and economic class from herself.

Joanna's diary.

October 1955
Today, somebody asked me what it was like being adopted. I said,"Fine. Why?" They told me they thought it must be odd not having my real Mum at home. I asked her how she knew I was adopted and she replied that her Mum had told her. Good job I knew . . . Mum said this might happen . . . but NO ONE ever mentioned it at Junior School.
When I got home I told Mum; she reassured me and made me promise not to worry. I asked Mum how I should reply if any other person mentioned it. She told me to tell them that I had been only 3 months old so couldn't remember a birth mother or father (TRUE) and as I had been legally adopted, I was now the child of MUM & DAD so it wasn't an issue.
Mum said that she could no longer remember any details, but she had some papers that I could have when I was older. She wanted to know if it bothered me not knowing who my mother was.
How could I be worried about such a thing? Mum & Dad are wonderful people and I love them with all my heart. I feel very lucky to have them as parents. I've got lovely cousins, grandparents, aunts and uncles so I shall never complain!

She was quite unaware of class distinctions and soon settled into her new school surroundings. Being gregarious, she was a loyal and enthusiastic member of every society that was on offer.

Catherine Dring—Martin, whose father was a reknowned business man in the town, was a 5' 3", twelve year old when Joanna joined her class. Joanna was a little girl of 4' 10" and at the age of ten became Catherine's pet.

On November the 5th, Catherine invited Joanna to the Dring-Martins' magnificent house on Wothorpe Drift, for a Fireworks Party. Patrick and Pamela wondered how to play the situation, for these people were people that they did not mix with. When her godmother Joan heard about it, she encouraged them to let Joanna go and 'see how the other half live'. It was arranged that Joanna, Pamela and Patrick would walk as far as town, Pamela would wait with Joan, who lived with her aged parents, whilst Patrick walked Joanna up to The Drift (as it was called by the hoi polloi). He would then, having delivered Joanna to the party, return to the house in town until the allotted time for collection of his daughter. In all, Patrick would walk about eight miles!! Was it worth it? Joanna thought so and Patrick enjoyed looking at the palatial house with its own swimming pool. It was a world far beyond the expectations of Patrick and Pamela, but they were delighted that they were giving Joanna a chance in life.

Work was challenging for her and she was anxious to give of her best, so Joanna spent many hours over homework. Eventually, her parents suggested that she gave up her beloved ballet and concentrate on piano lessons and school work.

When she was thirteen years old, in Upper IVB, she had a new form teacher, who came to teach Religious Education (R.E.) She was a dowdy lady, with grey hair, which was pulled behind her ears. Her facial hair was a recipe for being made a subject of ridicule. To make matters worse, she stumbled over her words and the girls soon began to make a note of the number of times that their teacher said 'er'. This usually ended for some unfortunate pupil staying in at break time to receive a reprimand because she could not control her giggles. Eventually, Joanna was summoned to the break detention. Miss Brightman smiled and said in a hushed tone,

"I am SO disappointed that you have found the need to join in with the other girls in their piece of fun."

Joanna immediately felt ashamed and hung her head, tears stinging her eyes.

"I know from Miss Hayes that you go to St. Mary's Church, so I thought I could rely on you to be caring and thoughtful."

Joanna did not know what to say. She looked up to find a smiling and understanding face.

"Well?"

"I'm sorry Miss, I won't do anything else again," she replied through her tears. "I'll try to stop the others too."

"Now that is a thoughtful way to go about things. Meanwhile, I think a letter of apology might be in order don't you?"

Joanna was dismissed, determined that she would be a more reliable pupil. In later years she realised that her punishment was just what she needed and often used it in her own teaching when it was appropriate.
Her friends wanted to know how the detention had panned out and Joanna said seriously,

"I think we may have been mean to her. I'm not going to count her 'er's any more and I'm going to listen a bit more."

Joanna soon learned that you do not keep friends or influence people if you decide to go against the norm, but she had a strong sense of right and wrong so stuck to her guns and soon discovered who her true friends were.

Whilst the other girls continued to laugh in the lessons when they had the task of colouring in the small paper booklets entitled 'Genesis', Joanna began to relish the opportunity to learn how biblical writings were influenced by oral tradition; to realise that the reason behind there being two stories of creation was based on the fact that one came from the North of the region and the other from the South. They were both in answer to the question 'Where did we come from?'. It was

a revelation to Joanna rather than a hinderance or laughing matter.
She persuaded her parents to buy her a Bible Commentary and began to read about the prophets and other writers. The girls eventually drove away the elderly Miss Brightman and a younger model was appointed to the post, in the hope that the pupils would regain respect and love for the subject.

Joanna was not only a religious girl, but was robust and good at sport. She represented her school at Netball and Rounders which meant three training sessions each week. She invariably had a Saturday morning match, Netball in the winter and Rounders in the summer. At the age of 14 she was playing 1st VII Netball and had trials for Lincolnshire, playing in the attacking centre position.

On Saturday afternoons, Joanna and Angela (her closest friend) went into town and enjoyed the newly opened coffee bar. Boarders from the boy's Direct Grant School in the town could be found there and a rapport was started between them.

For Valentine's Day, Joanna sent a card to Mike, who had shown some interest in her. He had also purchased a card, written a letter inviting her to the fair and sent a red rose. Joanna was beside herself with excitement and as Angela had also got a date at the fair, they made their way to the dodgems where they were to meet the boys. At the end of the evening, after an exciting time, they made their way along Broad Street to meet Mr. Henderson, who had come to collect Joanna.

"May I take Joanna home, Sir?" asked Mike.

Mr. Henderson was so impressed with this polite boy that he agreed to the request. He was soon to find that Mike was a regular visitor to the Henderson household. Being a boarder, he took many risks to be with his new girlfriend, but was never caught. When a roll call was imminent a mate would run round to the Henderson's house to fetch him. This was Joanna's first love and despite Mike being four years older than she was, he was shy and innocent. Nothing untoward came of the relationship and she was spared the traumas experienced by her unknown family.

Pamela, remembering the warning curse that her old neighbour had bestowed on them, decided that she had better lay down some stringent rules for Joanna to abide by, so that she would not be pregnant before marriage. One of these rules was that she was to bring home all boyfriends rather than meet them outside the home. Joanna was an amenable girl, and never thought to question her mother's demands. She told her mother everything about her relationship with Mike and he was encouraged to stay over during the holidays.

Her godmother, Joan, had introduced her to the church that she attended and Joanna soon became a regular member of the congregation at the High Anglican Mass each Sunday. Her faith became even more important to her and Joanna was confirmed at the age of thirteen. She committed herself to God in an enthusiastic manner.
She often went to Sunday lunch with the unmarried Joan and her parents. They taught her how to use cutlery correctly and introduced her to unusual dishes which they ate as starters, such as the steamed Yorkshire pudding batter served with lashings of delicious gravy, which was eaten before the roast dinner. Joan and her parents were rather old-fashioned and despite being richer than most people in Stamford, rancid butter was often used on the bread at tea-time. Joanna's parents always came to collect her after Sunday dinner and stayed to tea.

"Bloomin' butter. Spoil a ship for a halfpenny," moaned Patrick every time.

Since Pamela's Uncle, who was bald and always wore a cap around the house, had retired and the family had moved 'along the street', visits and meals were more frequent.

Joan also rationed the chocolates to one per picking. A box lasted a very long time and the chocolates had sometimes lost some of their colour. This bothered The Hendersons, but not Pamela's aunt, uncle or cousin!!

As Joan had no children of her own, Joanna became increasingly important to her and she taught her to cook and sew whenever they were alone. Joan even booked a holiday in Horncastle for them when Joanna was seventeen and they enjoyed each other's company, taking long walks along the beach and exploring the surrounding towns and villages.

In the school summer term, Lord Burghley (who was the chairman of the governors of the school) allowed the girls to spend their lunch breaks in his grounds. It was a chance to chat and laugh without being told to 'keep down the noise' or 'you are ladies, not hooligans'.
Joanna and her close in-school friends—Prudence, Judith, Veronica, Janet and Kathleen—all enjoyed these times, especially as few lived in the town and the only time they were able to see each other out of school hours involved a bus trip. Secrets, fears and hopes were shared and none of them could imagine life without each other! Little did they know how diverse their lives would be.

Joanna attended the Church Youth Club which met each Sunday after Evensong in a property owned by her Godmother. She 'courted' a number of boys, played mixed hockey, worked reasonably hard at school, and thoroughly enjoyed her teenage years.

At the age of fifteen she fell head over heels for a boy who attended the church during holidays. He was another boarder at Stamford School, but had relatives in the town with whom he stayed out of term time. Joanna and Steven soon became inseparable and they both found that love is a powerful force when you are young. When she went home with a 'love bite' on her neck, Joanna's mother read the riot act and she forbade her to meet her boyfriend again. At first, they ignored her, but one day, Mrs. Henderson was waiting at the 'arranged' meeting place, ordered Joanna home and threatened Steven that she would report him to his house master.

Joanna was bereft. She could neither work or sleep and as a result, failed four of the 'O' levels that she was taking although she passed Religious Education and English

Language and English Literature with flying colours. It was her first lesson in the price of love!

Most pupils were shepherded into Lower V1 General to redo exams in November, but as Joanna was so young, the school decided to put her into Upper V-1 to take five more subjects that could be added to the four she had already gained. With these qualifications it would mean that she could go into the sixth form to take 'A' levels in readiness for Teacher Training.

At the end of their fifth year, Janet left school to pursue farming with her parents, Kathleen and Judith went to work in a bank, Veronica became a model and Prudence stayed on in the sixth form. The in-school friends were spread, never to be together again.

By seventeen Joanna was involved with a boy from the church who met with the family's approval. She wasn't sure that he was the one for her, and at one point, Joanna decided that she wanted to sever relations with Julian, but his father died and she felt it would be mean to finish with him at the time. The courtship continued.

As he was at university, she was able to concentrate on her 'A' Levels of History, English and RE. Joanna decided she wanted to teach, but did not know whether to go to University or Teacher Training College. She felt that she was called to teach RE, so this became her main subject of study, with English and Dance as her subsidiaries.

Apart from listening to her father, and refusing a place to read Theology at Birmingham University she made only one mistake when she left home and went to Teacher Training College—she did not leave her older boyfriend behind. Being a loyal person by nature, she waited for the monthly visits from him instead of enjoying the camaraderie of others and fully experiencing College life.

Joanna remained very religious and enjoyed debating her views with others. It was a Diocesan college under the direction of the university and every student was made to attend seminars for English, Religious Studies and Education, as well as studying a main and subsidiary subject.

Joanna found herself in an accommodation hall, with a Warden. It was new and well appointed on the main site of the college. There were three storeys in each block and six rooms on each storey. Joanna loved her bright new room which not only had windows but a balcony. She customized her room not realizing she would not be spending the full three years there. The downside was that it was three miles from the Student Union building and other halls of residence.

On the first evening, the new students were invited to meet with the 'Block Rep'. She was a third year, who introduced herself and other third year students and acquainted them with the rules which were in force. On the second night, the new students decided to meet in the largest room on their floor to find out more about their neighbours.

"I loved reading 'Girl' and 'The Children's Newspaper', said Joanna, 'I learned so much about the goings on in the world and famous people of history."

"Yes," said Jean. "That's where I got my love for History and here I am with it as my main subject."

"And me," added Carol. "What are you two reading as your main subjects?"

"Music," said Linda.

"Me too," added Rosalind.

Christine was a more reserved girl and hadn't entered the conversation, so Joanna turned to her questioningly.

"I'm doing History as well," she beamed. "What is your main?"

"Divinity," replied Joanna.

There was a slight hush amongst the new friends, as few young people were engaged with religion or the church. The silence was broken by Rosalind, who told everyone that her father was a Headmaster in a Church School in a small village outside Stratford-upon-Avon.

Joanna was determined to return to the original topic of favourite reads and was interested to know if the other girls had used their town library.

"Oh yes," replied Christine. "I think I've read every Enid Blyton ever written."

"My Mum hated her," laughed Rosalind.

"Mine only reads rubbish love stories," said Joanna, "but she always encouraged me to read, as long as there wasn't a job that needed doing, or I was not using a torch under the bed clothes!"

"Oh, I always did that!" laughed Carol.

"And me," said Linda and Rosalind in unison.

"My Canadian cousin sent me 'Nancy Drew Mysteries' for birthdays and Christmas. Think that must be why I like crime," laughed Joanna.

"Let's tell each other what we like doing other than reading," suggested Jean.

"OK," replied Linda, "You start."

"Well, I love music—particularly The Beatles. I've brought my record player with me so we'll be able to listen to some of their records. What about you Joanna?"

"Well, I really like music, dancing and collecting. I've got cuttings from newspapers and comics that I stick into scrapbooks. I'll fetch one and show you," she said, getting up and running next door to her room.

She came back, carrying her precious possession which had articles on Grace Kelly's wedding to Prince Ranier of Monaco, The Mau Mau retaliation against the British in Kenya, with pictures of their leader, Jomo Kenyatta, and articles about the first communist government in the

Western Hemisphere, Cuba, and Fidel Castro. Interspersed with these were photographs of her family and friends, which were taken in the appropriate years when the events took place.

"Gosh!" exclaimed Christine. "I haven't ever done anything like that."

"I've got photos of my family and friends," said Jean, getting up and going to her book shelf. She took down a beautifully leather-bound album, which made Joanna's scrapbook from Smiths look rather paltry.

"It's not quite as personal as your book, Joanna, but it does have photos of the family and my friends—look at these of Dan, my boyfriend."

The girls duly gazed and asked questions, sharing snippets about their own families, friends and lives during pre college days. They talked about films, film stars and what they found interesting. Joanna told them how she had loved the voice of Vincent Price on the television, but had not enjoyed the macabre or horror that was associated with the star; she was more content with hearing him interviewed than appreciating his acting prowess.

They soon realised that they had spent two and a half hours talking about themselves, their aspirations, loves, hates and interests, in an attempt to get to know each other more deeply. Eventually, the new students decided to go back to their rooms in order to sleep in readiness for the new day. An Education day of lectures was on the agenda and they were all anticipating an exciting time, for they were aspiring teachers, anxious to learn about their chosen career.

As she reflected on her childhood after the evening with her new compatriots, Joanna realised that she had been well guided and cared for by her wonderful parents. They had ensured that she had received a good education and encouraged her talents. They had given her a good grounding in morals and the rights of all and had instilled in her a sense of self-worth. She had been encouraged to show kindness and consideration to others, without losing the fundamental belief and conviction within her own soul.

Perhaps she was rather too serious in her outlook on life and too 'straight' to try out the temptations that life offered. In fact, she was appalled when she heard that a girl in another hall had purchased a double sleeping bag for she and her boyfriend to share when they went away on a camping holiday in the summer holidays! Joanna could not imagine enjoying that sort of intimacy with anyone prior to marriage. She was unsure as to the meaning of the phrase 'getting carried away' and was always conscious that her mother had suggested that 'there would be real trouble' (whatever THAT meant) if she became pregnant. Joanna was probably going to be seen as rather straight-laced, but she would rather that be the label than 'slut' or 'easy-lay', which seemed to have entered the vocabulary since the television had become many people's bible for life.

Chapter 15   Marriage

At the end of her first year at college, Julian, aged 23 and
a half, asked Joanna's father if they could be married.
Joanna and Julian went into Peterborough and a beautiful
solitaire diamond was purchased as Joanna's nineteenth
birthday present. Julian tried to persuade his fiancee to have
a second-hand ring, but she chose a neat, simple ring, which
she felt fitted her personality. It had been arranged that
the marriage was to take place as soon as her training was
completed. He would be 25years old; an age he had always
decided on as being a good age to marry.

In her second year Joanna moved into digs in the town along
with another girl who had a boyfriend. Their idea was that
it would be easier to go away at weekends or have visitors.
It transpired that landladies in those days, when the age
of majority was 21, were as strict as House Wardens and
life was no easier. To make matters worse, Joanna's friend
received a letter from her boyfriend telling her that he had
met someone else. Tears and drinking bouts followed and
Joanna was required to give lots of support, whilst juggling
life between Julian and college.

In the Spring term of the second year, Joanna was elected
Chapel Warden so was expected to move into a specific room
in a specific lodge for her final year. It was a superb room,
which had a glorious outlook, so Joanna felt content. She
enjoyed her duties as Chapel Warden, preparing for her final
exams and entertaining new friends that she had met in main
buildings.

There were a lot of men whom she had not come across
whilst at New College. Being an attractive girl with a
ready smile and vivacious disposition, she found that she
was having offers of dates. She did not succumb to any,
although she found one boy very enticing. He needed
someone to dictate his long essay in order to get it finished
in time. He was recovering from a broken heart and Joanna
was engaged, so he felt safe to suggest that she helped

him out. They worked together every afternoon for two months—Joanna perched on the radiator, which was not blasting out heat on account of it being the summer, whilst Roger scribbled away from her dictation from his notes. Joanna was worried. She was beginning to let this man wander into her thoughts, and he told her that as she was engaged, he could not enter into a relationship with her, although he liked her a lot.

She went home at half term, feeling very confused.

She had doubts about her forthcoming marriage but when she voiced them to her parents she was assured that they were pre-marital nerves and her father told her that she would be fine, especially as the invitations had gone out!

So, the wedding went ahead as planned in the summer of 1966, despite Joanna's many misgivings. She knew that she felt no passion for Julian and she was unsure about her love for him. She thought he was a great friend and she loved the fact that they both had such strong feelings about religion—Roger was a non-believer, despite making her stomach churn when she was in his presence. Perhaps God would help her to weather any storms. She comforted herself with the fact that she had been told that sex was over-rated.

Julian and Joanna had a magnificent wedding with all the pomp and circumstance that accompanies the High Anglican tradition. She made a pretty bride, wearing a simple, straight white gown, which contrasted well with her auburn curls and her big, flashing, green eyes. She had three bridesmaids, dressed in the same simple style, in lemon. Her two pageboys wore lemon shirts and dark green trousers.

She was a virgin at the time of her marriage—Julian had insisted that their friendship was the best reason to tie the knot and that a white wedding would symbolise the purity of their love. It was a nuptial mass and the priest from the church that she had attended whilst at college gave the sermon—not that Joanna heard a word of it!

The reception was held in The Old Assembly Rooms and was a modest buffet. Julian drank and hardly ate anything and

Joanna did her best to circulate between the two families, who obviously were not impresssed with each other. The families sat on opposite sides of the room as though they had never met before or someone had a disease that must be avoided. Perhaps they could forsee the pitfalls that were to come. The newlyweds travelled to Manchester in the back of a bridesmaid's car, sitting either side of the priest who had given the sermon at the marriage service. Joanna felt that this was not how she had envisaged going on honeymoon, but kept her own counsel. On arrival at the hotel, Julian announced that they were to be up at six in order to board the flight to Newcastle.

"Why are we flying to Newcastle?" asked Joanna.

The 'butch' girl, who had lived in the room below her at college was a PE specialist and had attended the daily mass at the local church with Joanna, had lived in Newcastle and she went home by train.

"We are honeymooning in Newcastle, County Down, Ireland," replied Julian with a smirk. "Doug says it's a beautiful place and we can go on lots of walks, and it won't be too expensive."

Doug was Julian's work colleague and often came into conversation as he was an older man with whom Julian was impressed.

Joanna had never flown before, but she enjoyed the experience and was captured by the scenery, which was splendid.

Joanna felt little passion for her husband and was too naive to realise that a frisson was necessary if a marriage was to work. The honeymoon was further blighted by the arrival of Joanna's early period. The long route marches that she was subjected to made her tired and unable to feel the love that she so desperately wanted to show to her new husband.

They returned to Stamford after the honeymoon, and after three days moved down to London, where they were to make their home.

Julian had found a flat in a leafy suburb, which was only a short walk from the Central Line and their route into the City. It was very pleasantly furnished and their elderly landlady lived in the downstairs part of the house. The living room had a white leather three piece cottage suite and a small coffee table. An old-fashioned dining table lay flat against the wall behind the door and three dining chairs were lodged under its leaves. The fourth chair in the set provided extra seating and was against the second wall in the room. The window looked out onto the long garden, which the owner had once cultivated. Now widowed, she employed a gardener "to keep down the weeds, my dear". She was a delightful person and soon mothered Joanna with daily cups of tea on her arrival home from work.

Julian's comment as he took his new bride into his arms was,

'The sofa isn't big enough for two, but at least there's another easy chair!'

Joanna should have realised that this was indicative of things to come, but she innocently replied,

'Oh, we can cuddle up together; it'll be cosy.'

Julian laughed. But, when it came to sitting down with a cup of tea a few minutes after they had explored their new home, he sat in the chair which had the view of the garden, whilst she was invited to sit on the 'cosy sofa'.

The huge room at the front of the flat was the bedroom. It housed a large double bed, an enormous oak wardrobe and matching chest of drawers.

Their love-making since their return from honeymoon had been gentle, because they had been in Joanna's parents' house until they could move into the flat. It was not how Joanna had expected it to be and passion (as she had witnessed on Television dramas) was still lacking. She could not help wondering if Julian had only married her because she was his 'best friend', rather than someone whom he desired. She did not really understand what was meant by 'being swept off your feet', as the only person for whom she had experienced obsessive thoughts had been the boyfriend whose departure had blighted her 'O' level results. Julian certainly did not make her feel like dissolving into his arms when he came into the room, but she loved him and decided that she must be sensible about her misgivings.

The young married couple immediately joined the local church. By Christmas they had become involved in running a Youth Club along with a bachelor who was to become a close friend.

Initially all was well, but Julian quickly became critical of Joanna.

August 1966
I'm having real problems. He hasn't let me go home and see Mum and Dad since we married and we are going to Stamford next month for a wedding, but they will be away on holiday so I won't see them then. He argues that I am HIS now and belong to him so I must cut the apron strings. WHY is he so difficult?

Unfortunately for his new wife, Julian did not like discussions. He was irascible and often flew into tantrums over what Joanna felt were 'important things', such as where they should sit in the evenings, what music should be played in the house, the dishes that Joanna served up for meals and what Joanna should do during her day off.

Being a 'best friend' was obviously insufficient for Julian. After one disastrous attempt at lovemaking, a few months into the marriage, he remarked, 'I would rather be with anyone other than you. You are USELESS in bed'.

Joanna felt devastated and did not know where to turn. How could she tell anyone that her husband thought that she was useless in bed and was full of disappointment with their marriage?

Julian was difficult to please in every area of life, (except in anything connected to the church), so when he complimented her on a meal that she had cooked, Joanna prepared it again. By the end of the week, they had eaten the same dish four times. Julian was not happy about this and suggested

Joanna learned another dish to cook. When she told her new-found friend on the staff, she realised that Julian had not approached the problem with a laugh, but had been judgemental and belittling. This was his manner and Joanna knew that she would have to learn to live with it.

Joanna's self-esteem was beginning to shrink beneath the constant scathing remarks of her husband and she gradually became a submissive wife in order to keep some harmony. Her satisfaction in life had to come from outside the marriage, which was not what Joanna had envisaged. She sought happiness through her pupils in the classroom and the young people who sought refuge three times weekly at the Church Youth Club.

She decided that 'making love' had been romanticised by the media and books. True happiness lay in helping others and using the talents that you had been given by God.

Despite their proximity to the city, the home of Carnaby Street and new ideas, Joanna did not go to the shops in Oxford Street or Regent Street until the first visit of her parents. She and Julian only crossed London to go to the Athletics Stadium at White City with their new-found friend from the Church Youth Club. It was as though Julian did not want them to be sullied by the experience of 'Swinging London' in the 60s or let it have any impact on their lives. Her husband was determined to live in 'an Edwardian England' and hold 'Edwardian views', so Joanna had no opportunity to enjoy the joys of life in the 1960s.

Joanna's first teaching post was with the Inner London Education Authority. The school was in Bethnal Green and she travelled to work on the tube's Central Line, changing at Mile End. Eventually, the landlady's son who lived nearby gave both Julian and his new wife a lift into The City, dropping off Joanna outside the Mile End station.

It was the days of mini skirts and Julian told her that her legs were 'for my eyes only, so don't even think about one'. This put her in a difficult position in a place where all young female teachers and adolescent boys expected a mini skirt. Each day, whilst she strap hung, Joanna turned over the waistband of her skirt so that she arrived dressed appropriately at the school.

She had married Julian 'for better or worse. in sickness and in health' and he was her husband. She must learn to accept her life and, with God's help, love him without any barriers. So, naturally, she became anxious when he did not return from work at a reasonable time.

Extracts from Joanna's diary

March 1967
Julian very late home. I phoned his work and got his boss. He told me there was prob. a delay on underground as J had left ages before. J home about twenty mins later. Cried; told him I'd been worried so had phoned office. He went MAD. Screamed that I was NEVER to do such a thing again. His working life was completely divorced from life with me. Said that the Church Youth Club made life bearable 'cause it took up so many evenings. Also said it would be better making love with a sack of potatoes as I was so frigid. Wondered if our marriage could have been a mistake, but goes on about 'for better or worse'. DEVASTATED.

She did not think anything else other than that she had invaded Julian's privacy, which made her feel dreadful and inadequate. Perhaps her marriage *had* been a mistake. When he showered criticism in his belittling manner one Thursday night, she made a decision: she could bear it no longer. She would go back home to her parents and admit that she had failed.

Two days later.
Well, that didn't work. Got as far as the corner post box and realised didn't have my purse with me. He was waiting at the gate. Grabbed me and hauled me upstairs. Have never been beaten over somebody's knee before. Cried and cried but he wasn't even sorry. Called me awful names and told me we'd have to grin & bear it. Not like I imagined—too much literature and television!

Chapter 16   Better Days

Joanna's teaching experience gave her much joy. She had
learned that some pupils aren't cut out for examinations. In
1966, however, all were expected to prepare for Certificate of
Secondary Education examinations. By the fifth year pupils
were questioning scientific theories against religious beliefs.
Asking them to produce a 'Project' with a religious theme as
a piece of course work created all sorts of difficulties. What
could one do about the disaffected delinquent?

Julian hardly listened to her stories connected to her days
at school. She had hoped that he might shed some ideas
about her dilemmas, but he was more concerned with his
Rugby strategies for the 'game on Saturday' than any of her
quandaries. She could have approached her Headteacher,
but did not want to be seen wanting and, as she was the only
RE teacher in the small secondary school, she was forced to
work from instinct.

Tommy was a wonderful non-coping teenager who was
constantly in trouble, both in and out of school. He was less
than interested in academia and had no place for religion
in his life. It was a difficult few lessons at the start of her
career and Joanna was beginning to fear that she had made
a mistake in her choice of subject. Discussing Tommy in the
staff room was not a problem, as his name was often in the
arena, so she probed deeper and discovered that he had some
artistic flair. With this in mind, she suggested to Tommy
that he could use paintings as his base for the project and
provide a line of explanation under the picture. Together
they decided that this may be the way forward and Tommy
felt that he could produce something that he might label
as 'A guide for children.' Eventually, 'Moses' was chosen
to be the target for this venture in painting, crayoning and
pencil drawing which began to appear. The explanatory
line beneath each picture caused far more heartache than
was complimentary to the artwork, but the finished article
was breath taking. Tommy did not gain a very high mark
for CSE, but he was presented with an award by the caring

Head Master, who recognised that a difficult pupil had succeeded in an area that had formally been alien to him throughout his schooling.

Joanna became deeply concerned for the slow learner and finding ways that they could access the curriculum. This maxim held her in good stead for the rest of her career.

Extracts from Joanna's diary

JUNE 1967

At least the kids are great. Had my assessment today. An old buffer came into the classroom when I had 5C. The kids were great and involved, raising their hands and answering questions. Sam even did some written work. The Inspector told me to continue in this way and I could go far! When I told Julian, he laughed and said, 'Don't bank on it. You'll never be any good if I'm not around.' Now, WHAT does that mean?!

JULY 1967

Ashmoor told me that he was pleased with my first year. The report from the Inspector was complimentary to all of us and we have passed and have become qualified teachers. There is talk of us getting together one evening, but I said I wouldn't be able to come in from Wanstead, because Julian didn't like me going out once he was home. We went out for a drink at the lunch hour to celebrate. They are a great bunch of people. When I told Julian that evening there was a huge row over the pub that we had chosen to drink in and he made me promise not to go out again. Actually, he won't let me do anything without him!
If I disagree he storms and raises his voice (the landlady heard a row last week and remarked on it) to the extent that he frightens me—and I remember the beating.

Two years down the line Joanna moved on to a Remedial department in Stepney Green and met some of the most challenging pupils of her career.

Stanley was very tiny for his years but made up for it by being extremely difficult in the classroom. He was attention seeking beyond all reason and caused as many distractions as possible. When the pupils arrived in the classroom, Stanley started to sing "You are the sunshine of my life . . .", wait for Joanna to sit down at the desk and promptly hop up into her lap. At first she was horrified and insisted he got down, but as his behaviour did not improve, Joanna decided one day to accept the situation and work from there. Everyone accepted this bizarre form of attention seeking—probably because they were able to learn something in a quiet way—and she was able to proceed with the lesson. After the first fortnight Joanna did not sit at her desk before delivering the introduction to the lesson and Stanley soon stopped demanding a place on her knee.

Linda was volatile and in the second year of Secondary school. She was one of twenty-seven pupils in the remedial class, very disturbed but usually co-operative. Joanna was congratulating herself for 'taming' this difficult group, but foolishly forgot the saying "pride comes before a fall." Taking a moment to sit at her desk and mark someone's work, instead of her usual meander around the room, she failed to see Linda leave her seat. One of the boys suddenly shouted,

"Miss. Quick. Look. Linda's crawling along the window ledge."

To her horror Linda was indeed doing so and appeared through the second open window. If you can imagine a three storey building and the room being on the second storey, you may experience the feelings that flowed through Joanna. When questioned, Linda explained that someone had dared her to do this dastardly act and she took the opportunity of Joanna's distraction to 'win' the dare. Both the boy who had egged on this child and Linda herself were severely reprimanded by the Head of Department and threatened with an exclusion if they even contemplated another stupid act. It would have been pointless in sending them home as there was no one in and the parents would have enjoyed the situation too much. The newspapers would have had a field day if she had fallen.

Being the only woman in the department Joanna was often in demand. On one famous—or perhaps it should read infamous—occasion she was sent for during the lunch hour. A renowned villain of the female species, Janice, had picked up a pile of plates and proceeded to smash them over the person who was in front of her in the dinner queue. Needless to say, there was some blood, flying fists and raised voices when Joanna arrived at the scene. She walked up to the fighting girls, opened her arms to the perpetrator and spoke soothingly. Janice burst into tears, flung herself into Joanna's arms and after a few moments of hushed silence in the room Joanna was able to lead her to safety.

After this incident Joanna built a reputation for being able to deal effectively with 'difficult' pupils, which remained with her for the whole of her teaching career.

December 1968
Has decided he wants to be a priest. I am to go home and live with my parents and get a job in a local school whilst he trains. WHAT?!!! He can't possibly love me so why continue? Too scared to do anything, but perhaps time away will heal our problems. May God guide us. Can hardly believe that it has all turned out like this. WHY? WHY?

February 1968
He's been accepted by Theological College and is very thrilled. So, Stamford here I come. Says he hates The City and all that it stands for. Thinks it will be easier when he is away from the fraud and corruption. He's probably right. I shall quite enjoy being a vicar's wife I expect. Meanwhile, I shall have to go back to Stamford with my tail between my legs. People just won't believe we are living apart whilst he trains . . . You just don't do that sort of thing. Whatever will the parents think? Perhaps his mother will give me some more domestic hints—don't know what I would have done if she hadn't taught me to patch—Julian's rugby clothes are always in the wars, as she predicted. My Mum's darning lessons have come in useful too thank goodness—J doesn't believe in wasting anything.

The next step was for Julian to be interviewed by The Bishop's Selection Panel and then he would be able to start his training for the ministry.
Julian set off in the middle of June for his two day interview in London. He felt confident and told Joanna that as he had a place at Chichester College there could be no problem.

July 1968
Hasn't been chosen by the panel, despite his place at college. He's devastated. Searching for a new SUITABLE job. He can't stay in the CITY

which he now finds intolerable. At least he appears to retain his sense of
proportion and balance about the world. Even cried with disappointment
and disbelief. Allowed me to comfort him over his disappointment, but
obviously anxious because we can't live like this any more.
Relieved that we shan't have to live apart. That would surely have been
the end of the road for us. Not sure how he feels about that.

Joanna suggested that Julian apply for different jobs which
might provide some purpose to their lives in London. She
felt very satisfied with her own position at the school in
Walthamstow and had even applied for a more senior post.
Unbeknown to her, Julian had his own ideas, which would
mean a move out of the Metropolis.

January 1969
Going to be HOUSEPARENTS for The Children's Society. Not sure how I
feel, but expect it'll be good. Have had to withdraw application for school/
liaison officer, which I would have liked, but as Julian has said, I shall be
able to do some worthwhile work with these children. Teaching in the East
End has been demanding, although have had some marvellous moments.

The Children's Society ran an 'apprenticeship' scheme so
that trainees moved from one centre to another working
alongside the houseparents.
Joanna and Julian's training was successful and they enjoyed
their placements—especially as their sleeping arrangements
meant that they were unable to share a bed!

After 6 months they were summoned to Headquarters and
offered a Home for fourteen children in Ipswich. There were
only eight in the Home initially, as the Housemother was
deteriorating in health and the Society had tried to ease the
burden for her and her husband.
Joanna and Julian had been surprised at the age of most of
the Houseparents; they were, by far, the youngest couple and
their attitude to situations was often more progressive than
some of the older stalwarts. Joanna's teaching experience
and their ability to deal with difficult adolescents, as was
proved in their running of a Church Youth Club in the
East End of London, meant they were soon allocated
more children to make up their quota. Generally, all went
smoothly, although Julian could write a book about the
problems that he encountered.

Their reputation went before them and they were soon acknowledged to be excellent carers. Children thrived under their protection and boys with difficulties became the norm in the house.

One day, Joanna opened the door to a boy of 17, who held a huge bouquet of flowers in his arms.

"Hello," he stammered. "I'm sorry, but you don't know me. I used to live here before I went into the Navy."

"Oh. Are you Trevor?" asked Joanna, who had heard tales of the boy who had found a niche in the forces.

"Yes," he answered. "They've slung me out of the Navy and I've nowhere to go."

"Well, come in. We'll see what we can do for you."

Joanna took Trevor into the sitting room and fetched Julian, who was fortunately talking on the phone to the House Social Worker. Julian asked if he would hold the line whilst he listened to Joanna's message.
Once the Social Worker heard about Trevor's return, he told Julian to keep him at the house until he was able to come across to Ipswich in a few hours from then.

Trevor had been caught stealing, which had meant instant dismissal. He had been shipped home, given his fare to Ipswich and told to make his way home. What could he do?

"I only have here," he sobbed.

"O.K. I'm sure we can work something out for you," he was promised.

Joanna asked one of the staff to make up a bed in the guestroom and Trevor stayed in the house for a month until a placement was secured for him with an elderly couple who had befriended him when he was a child.

'Hands' arrived complete with sword, tapes, books, motorbike and 'HANDS' in metal studs across a black leather jacket. He was a towering six-foot four and dwarfed the houseparents who met him at the door with the Social Worker. A BOWAVTA (boarding out with a view to adoption) break-down, he looked like trouble.

Julian put out his hand and removed the sword from his grasp. "Where did you get this?" he asked.

"The Museum," answered the 'cool dude' standing before him.

"We'll return it tomorrow, when you have settled in."

Joanna organised a locker for him in the sitting room, rather than the playroom, where the younger children had lockers for their private use. As he filled it with his belongings, she noticed that there were three books in his possession which all bore the same title.

"Why three?" she asked.

"Lifted," was the reply.

Momentarily lost for words, Joanna squeaked, "Right. Don't do it again."

It transpired that 'Hands' had removed books, tapes, sweets and any movable object that could be 'lifted' during his seventeen years of life. He told Joanna that he had taken sweets from the counter as he left the shop at which he had a newspaper round.

"No one ever noticed, despite me having them sticking out of my top pocket."

"Did you want someone to see them?" Joanna asked.

"Sure. They could have stopped me, couldn't they?"

That night, Joanna and Julian spent their time discussing the minds of vulnerable children with no guidance from parents, and were determined to give their 'family' as good a start as possible.

Joanna thanked God that she had been adopted and given the chance to fulfil her potential. How lucky she had been!

'Hands' stayed with the family until he married a girl who was half his size and bearing his child. They moved into a little house in town and had three further children, who were supported by The State and 'Hands' part-time job as a builder's mate.

Within a year, the Society's family had grown to sixteen children and the Houseparents had employed two more residential staff, a cleaner and a laundry lady.

The committee members visited each month. Joanna was never reluctant to put forward her case for new clothes (the children had previously worn 'hand-me-downs', which had other children's names written in the waistband or collar) and better bedrooms and facilities for her brood, and she gradually became respected for her beliefs.
Most of the time Joanna felt happy, except on those occasions when Julian said something belittling to her in front of others. That made her cry.

After Julian's rejection by the Church, they had stopped attending services and being involved with organised religion, and the children were told that they could choose to go to Sunday school if they so wished. Some did. Others decided that a game of football or reading their books was more to their liking.

Television was important to the children. With their former Houseparents it had been an opportunity to spend time watching programmes and making comments about them to each other. In 1967 they had been given a colour television by the Americans, who were on the base near Ipswich. Watching BBC2 they had enjoyed the first live broadcast from inside a US Space capsule in orbit. 'Dad's Army' was a favourite of the older ones in the house. They had all experienced Neil Armstrong's moonwalk, either live or on news bulletins in 1969.

It was an exciting time for the world and even for the small community organised by Julian, with a little help from Joanna, in Ipswich.

More personal excitement was on the horizon.

Extract from Joanna's diary.

May 1971
Think I may be pregnant.

Three days later.
I am . . . Julian seems to be as pleased as I am. Informed HQ and they told J that it was really good for the children if the Houseparents had children. My parents and J's mother seem to be delighted at the prospect of being grandparents . . . Not going to tell the house 'family' until a few more months have passed. Will have to go to docs every month and he is going to arrange for me to have baby in a small cottage hospital in town. Told me to rest every pm, so the burden is going to fall on J but he says he won't mind.

September 1971
Some of the children reacted badly to the news of a baby. Jenny said SHE would kill it as she wanted our time and Andrew said HE would help her cos he HATES his brother and sister. Oh dear, what will happen? Some of them are SO disturbed.

Sophie was born to Joanna and Julian in December 1971, so entries in Joanna's diary stopped for some years.

There were many problems once the Houseparents had a child of their own. It would probably have been workable had it not been for the regular threats to their baby daughter from some of the disturbed youngsters in their care.

Joanna left Sophie to sleep in the bedroom one morning because the children were home for half term. Some of the 'family' went to Special Schools which catered for disturbed beings. Some of them had many problems in their heads, which made caring for them during holidays a challenging task.

When Joanna reached the kitchen where she was going to prepare mid-morning drinks for everyone, Robert, who was ten years old, was pouring the kettle of water over a doll in the toy pram.

"What are you doing, my dear?" Joanna asked, knowing the answer before he gave it.

"I'm killing Sophie."

"Oh. Why is that?"

"You're always with her and not with us."

"Well I'm here now. And so is Auntie Ann (who had come into the kitchen whilst Joanna was talking)."

"Come with me into the playroom with the others," said Ann, taking the little boy's hand, "we'll see what the others are doing. I'm sure you'll be able to join in."

Joanna went to the office to find Julian. She burst into tears.

"Come on, old thing," said Julian getting up and putting his arms round his fragile wife.

He had recognised that she needed care after the birth of their child and had been very supportive of her, taking the burden of running a children's home onto his own shoulders in order to give his wife time with the baby.

"What ever is wrong? Is Sophie alright?"

"Yes," she hiccoughed, "I found Robert in the kitchen pouring water over a doll in the toy pram."

"Ah," sighed Julian. "I can guess what he said. Where is he now?"

"With Auntie Ann and the others in the playroom. She came in and heard most of what he said, so she is well aware and will tell Shirley."

After this episode, Julian decided that they should work a more pro active system, which included the members of Staff working together when all the children were at home on holidays. He devised a shift system where Julian and Joanna worked as a team and Ann and Shirley were the other team, with an overlap in order to pass on information, when the children were at school.

Julian also decided that they needed to buy a house nearby now that they were a proper family, so that he, Joanna and Sophie could spend their days off away from the house.

Joanna's health was taking a battering. She became increasingly anxious when the children were at home and over-protective of her small baby. Julian drove his wife and child to Stamford regularly, so that they could both relax and enjoy their new, precious child with the grandparents.

The marriage was *existing*. Unlike many husbands, Julian rarely allowed time for them to be alone together. Professionally, they were an excellent team but there was little romance in their relationship. Joanna felt sure that she had only become pregnant because they had enjoyed a short holiday in Devon and had been 'more loving' than usual. Sex was not a feature of their lives and usually, one or other was too tired, because of the demands of their job to spend hours in bed if not using the time to sleep.

Her parents, mother-in-law, sister-in-law and friends were constant visitors to the house and Julian was able to concentrate on his role as Housefather; after all, as he often told everyone, he was in the position of doing the work of two.

The Doctor was extremely kind and helpful and Joanna made a good recovery with the help of Valium and medical care.

All was going well when the government decided to abandon children's homes and this changed the policy of the Society. After much telephoning, discussions with Social Workers and liaison with Local Authorities over three months, most of the children were restored to their own parents. Some were placed in foster homes. It was a heartrending time for many.

HQ had meetings with Julian and the Local Authority and it was initially thought that the house might be converted to a home for single mothers. At the request of his bosses in London, Julian made plans to change the configuration of the existing house so that he and his family could live 'separately' away from the mothers and children, but in the same building. At the last moment, the Society decided to sell the property and build a new, modern house for the project.

Julian and Joanna came out of child-care in 1974 and started a family life in Essex with Sophie and a foster son, Steven—the only child that they could not place or return to his birth family. Julian rejoined an old work colleague who had started his own business in London. Joanna, however, felt that he chose to go back to The City, which he allegedly hated, so that he could have long days away from her and the children. Their lives were almost separate.

When Sophie was four years old and her brother had left school, Joanna returned to work in a private school that would pay her by the day. The Head agreed to have Sophie in the school and deducted 50p from Joanna's wages to pay for Sophie's education. She was an asset to the school and proved to be highly intelligent, which was a delight for her parents. Steven had been accepted by The Forestry Commission and was training with them at their college whilst working in the local forest. He was offered a house at the edge of the forest and as long as Joanna continued to do his washing, supply him with food, visit him with Sophie and allow him home regularly, all was well.

Soon, Julian became bored of London life and announced that they would be moving to the Midlands. He had a new and better job. Neither Sophie's schooling or Joanna's teaching job was considered. Steven was established and Julian felt that it would be the 'making of him' if he had to fend completely for himself.

He had made the decision without any consultation. This was to be a pattern for their life from now on.

Despite having a beautiful daughter and a wonderful son, Joanna realised that she was committed to a lifetime of personal unfulfilment.

Julian thought so too. He was a good provider and was highly committed to his children, but hardly hid his growing dislike for his wife. He worked for a growing firm in a nearby village, and although he should have been able to return for lunch each day, as he had promised before they moved, Julian always found an excuse to stay away.

After three days of supply teaching at the local Primary School, Joanna understood why her daughter was so happy. It was a thriving school which was well managed. The Headmaster had surrounded himself with attractive, mature, experienced teachers, who had personality to burn. When a permanent post was advertised, Joanna applied. Although nervous, she knew she had a lot to offer and played to her strengths. The Headmaster had been impressed when she had done supply teaching for him, so was delighted that she had applied for the vacant post. Within two days, a letter dropped onto the doormat and Joanna was able to be happy again and not fret that her husband did not come home for lunch or arrive home before six o'clock each evening.

Her teaching job at the local school was the salvation for Joanna. She was a successful teacher and was able to engage the most difficult pupil in the classroom.

During her first term at the school, she had been astounded when the Headmaster came into the room on Parent's Evening with his wife. She had not realised that she was teaching his daughter in her class and was amazed at the details that the little girl had taken home to her parents. At the suggestion of the Headmaster, she moved 'the naughty table' to the back of the room, away from her desk, because one of the deprived boys was deliberately being naughty in order to sit near her!

Sophie accompanied her to school as it was in walkable distance, being only across the recreation ground. She continued to be an outstanding pupil, always eager to learn and had her father's ability to remember facts and her mother's aptitude for number and problem solving. Steven continued to progress in The Forestry Commission and was soon taking advanced courses in order to better himself. He enjoyed his monthly visits and returned home with his clean laundry.

Joanna knew that she had an affinity with the slow learner and became very interested in the work offered by a visiting teacher, to the three boys with reading difficulties. With a change of Headteacher came a change of approach to learning. He suggested that his Staff went on a course to see how one could offer a curriculum to each child at his own level.

Joanna was inspired. She developed individual programmes for each of her pupils—some tasks were undertaken by small groups and some were a whole class input. The Head was delighted when he visited the classroom. He saw two boys painting, a small group plodding through an English exercise, others reading or experimenting with seeds and another group completing a Mathematical problem.

Although demanding, Joanna found a great deal of satisfaction in her work. Sophie was making good progress at school, and Joanna had no feelings of guilt at working hard during the evenings when she prepared extra work for the slower learner. Sophie often helped with drawings or labelling when she had completed her homework, or had become bored with her television or computer.

Sometimes, Joanna felt that she and Julian were each like single parents, rarely communicating with the other and never considering a family life. She was worn out with trying to keep a family together and Julian's constant belittling of her was becoming unbearable. He was so self-righteous that she found being with him repulsive.

Joanna knew their lives were drifting apart. Love of their children seemed to be the only thing they had in common. This, however, cannot sustain a marriage.

Chapter 17   There Is Hope

With three children, Norma's application for a council house was accepted. The family moved into a three bedroomed house on an estate near to the town centre when Amanda was two years old. Norma enjoyed making a home for her family and again put her talents to work in making a special place for them to grow and blossom. She soon had new curtains, adjusted from the ones that had hung in the flat, a highly polished table with matching chairs, which her mother helped her to bid for at a sale, and bedding which she sewed lovingly, fit for her prince and princesses. There was a garden that the children could play in and she had many ideas to make it attractive, mixing wild plants with the formal plants expected of a garden. She was determined that her children would not suffer from having only one interested parent.

"How was school?" she asked of her eldest child as he flopped into the chair on return at the end of the day.

"I HATE it," he replied, bursting into tears.

"Why my love?" asked his anxious mother, putting her youngest onto the sofa, "what happened?"

"They called me a sissy and said I was coloured," sobbed Alexis.

"We'll sort it tomorrow," proclaimed his mother, "you sit with your sisters and watch Children's Hour whilst I get us some nice tea. Would you like toast with a bit of bacon tonight?"

"Oh yes please," Alexis sobbed through his tears, whilst his older sister rubbed his arm affectionately.

Having spent a restless and mainly sleepless night, Norma stormed up to school in defence of her small boy and demanded that something was done to help her distressed child.

"Why don't you suggest that he calls himself Alex, which is the english version of his name, so that the children won't make fun of that. That will be a start."

"OK," replied Norma, who thought it might be a good idea as he had been named after his father, who rarely had contact with his children, "and will you speak to the children who are being mean to him?"

"I certainly will, Miss Jackson. It *is* difficult when children live differently from their peers. Children can be much more cruel than adults because they are outspoken and say what comes into their heads."

"Or are repeating what they hear at home. My children are as good as anyone else's and you will never see them neglected or hungry. EVER!" snapped Norma.

"We know that, Miss Jackson, and we are impressed with the way Alex is sent to school; so you need have no worries. We are on YOUR side. I'll speak to the pupils responsible for making Alex unhappy and if you come in to see me in a couple of days, we'll review the situation. OK?"

"OK. Thank you, Miss Armstrong. Thank you," replied Norma, picking up her bag and preparing to leave.

"Have you given the girls English names?" asked the Head.

"Oh yes. As it happens I have."

"Probably a good thing then," smiled Miss Armstrong, "are they with friends at the moment?"

"Oh yes, thank you," replied Norma, hurrying off.

She was beginning to feel that the Head Mistress was asking too many personal questions for her liking. Norma had left the girls at the corner shop with the lady who owned it and who had often shown her kindness rather than judgement, which she felt from many sources when she went into town. After the arrival of her third child Norma's father had become increasingly hostile towards her. Her mother's health was deteriorating and she was less able to support Norma as she had done when William transported her. Amy told her that he was punishing Norma in retaliation for what had happened during the war. Although William did not mention the time, he was very voluble about young women who had affairs or were unmarried mothers.

"Never says anything if it's a man," Amy smirked to her daughter, "think he must hate women deep down. But he's OK—and we exist quite nicely. He's kind to me when I have a bad day. In fact, he's kinder since I was diagnosed than he was when he first came back from the war. Mind you, when you think about it, he had every reason to be upset, hadn't he?"

"There were HUNDREDS of women in that position," replied Norma, "and I expect some didn't get pregnant."

"Hum," smiled Amy, "and I guess they aren't all as fertile as you and me, eh?"

Norma laughed and tried to move the conversation on to other topics.

"But I'm very careful now," said Amy seriously. "I let him have his own way a lot, in order to keep the peace and I'm very grateful for the way he looks after me. I can't manage without him, so perhaps you could try and forgive him for not being understanding . . . And get yourself a man and have a life for yourself."

"That's not as easy as it sounds, mother. I hardly go out and I can't get a proper job until Andrina goes to school, but watch this space then," she laughed.

When her mother had left that day, Norma began to think about what she had said. She realised that her mother understood her husband and Norma's own predicament, so she knew that Amy could only give a little support now and then. She vowed she would try to like her father more, but she held bitter resentment towards him for the difficult times in her early life, the beatings that he had given her and her beloved mother and the lack of warmth that he had shown to her or her children. She vaguely understood why he had

142

thrown her out of the family home when she had become
pregnant so early in her life, but his unrelenting hostility to
them all was hard to come to terms with.

Norma ensured that life was never boring for herself or her
children and encouraged them all to help in the kitchen,
taught them to cook and clean the house, wash and always
look presentable so that they could mix with everyone and
not see themselves as inferior to anyone.

When her youngest child was old enough to go to school,
Norma returned to work and was able to buy a few luxuries
for the family. She knew that her feelings for Alexis would
always be the same, but was determined to bury him under
her work in order to provide for their children.

Norma worked hard and was soon able to afford driving
lessons. She was a natural driver and passed the test easily.
Her father decided that he would show some kindness to
her because she had been more thoughtful to him in recent
times, so he bought her a small car, which became almost as
important to her as her wonderful children.

They had settled into school life and Alice had become an
outstanding pupil, with a special talent for Art and Craft.
She was a charming girl and had lots of friends, whose
families accepted her and her situation, so Norma had little
to worry about where she was concerned.

Alex still had a few issues because he was not 'sporty'.
His work and disposition had improved since attending
Secondary school and he seemed much happier in himself.
However, he often asked about his father, whom he
remembered fondly. The girls had barely known him, but
Alex knew he was capable of playing with a child and
showering love on it when the mood took him—and it had
done when he visited his son and his mother in the early
sixties!

Andrina was stubborn and difficult. Norma was unsure as to
why but wondered if three children, the desertion of Alexis
and the problems she had faced bringing up three 'fatherless'
children had impacted on her youngest child. Her mother

said that she thought Andrina had inherited William's genes and that was why she was sometimes challenging. This made the women smile, but did not ease the burden that Norma carried.

"You'll have to get out and meet some handsome fellow. Those children need a man's touch now that they are getting on," encouraged Amy.
"Isn't there anyone at work?"

"Well . . ." replied Norma.

"You'll have to set your cap at him. I'm sure you could . . . if you're anything like I was in my day!!"

She was twenty eight. James Hill had joined the firm as a junior director a month earlier. He was handsome, witty and charming and soon won the hearts of the 'girls' in the office.

He eventually asked Norma to go out on a date, and as she felt that she had allowed sufficient time to elapse, she arranged for her mother to baby-sit for her, bought a new dress and perfume and prepared to enjoy herself again.

"I knew you could get someone if you tried," her mother had said when asked to baby-sit the children.

Norma had not been aware that she had tried to get James interested in her, although she had looked in his direction and always been kind and willing to carry out tasks asked of her. She had not known what she had done when she had been asked out by Alexis, but her friends had told her that she was a natural flirt and used her eyes very cleverly. She had laughed at their suggestion, but it had worked then and was obviously working now!

James seemed undeterred by Norma's revelation about her ready-made family and continued to date her. Norma introduced him to the children and her parents, who all seemed to like him. They decided not to wait long before marrying as time was running away with their lives. A small wedding at the register office was arranged and Norma waited anxiously for her future husband to arrive. She wondered if James would decide that he was not ready for marriage and commitment as Alexis had done twelve years earlier, but James and Norma were duly married and the Hill family began their life together.

Norma had insisted that they stay in the house, which suited James, as he realised that it would cost more money than he had to buy a house big enough for them all. He had only one condition. The children were to be adopted by him so that they could live as a proper family. Everyone was delighted with this idea and the legality was finalised one May morning in 1972.

For the first two years life was idyllic. One day, Alex needed reprimanding, and although James normally left the discipline to Norma, on this particular day, he was feeling raw and before anyone realised, he lashed out at the teenager. Norma was horrified and tried to interject, but James turned his hand on her. When she next met up with her mother, Norma was nursing the vestiges of a black eye.

"Whatever has happened to you?" enquired Amy with concern.

"Oh! Walked into the door," she tentatively replied.

"Now, don't give me that," said her mother firmly. "Has he been bashing you about?"

Norma dissolved into tears and her mother put her arm around her shoulder.

"I see. And how often is this animal hurting you?" asked Amy.

"No more often than dad ever did to us both."

"They're all the same," said Amy, bitterly.

"Was your American man like that?"

"Well, no . . . but we never lived together, and it was war time, so you can't really judge it can you?"

"Alexis never hit me, but he knew how to hurt me. At least the bruises will go, but you can never get rid of memories."

"You're worth more than that, Norma, so don't let James hurt you. Send him on his way if things get unbearable. It would be better to be without him than take the beatings . . . Has he hurt the children?" she asked anxiously.

The thought of her beloved grandchildren being abused by anyone was completely alarming. She had always loved children and would not contemplate hurting a hair on their heads. Amy had always believed in gentle discipline to keep things on an even keel, but would never slap unnecessarily. Not like William, who had been too ready with his fists and admonishment of both herself and her beautiful Norma.

"He turned on Alex the other evening, but I don't think he has touched the girls," Norma replied.

"Oh dear," fretted Amy, "it's history repeating itself. Don't let him stay if he's beating you all."

Because Norma's father had hit both her mother and herself, she had accepted that this is what happened in marriage. Thinking about it later, Norma suspected that James *was* guilty of abusing all her children, but she had no proof. She had not witnessed anything untoward, other than the time when James had slapped Alex. She was too alarmed by James' fury to get between him and his hand. Could their lives be in danger? She could not understand why he had changed so much. Norma began to wonder if there was a defect in her nature, which ensured that men would not stay constant where she was concerned.

However, the slaps and beatings of herself became commonplace. Norma found that there were days that she was unable to attend work because of the visible bruises. The day came when she decided that she would be forced to confront her husband when he came home and after the children were safely in bed.

Norma took a deep breath.

"This can't go on. I'm becoming a nervous wreck. I never know if you're going to be calm when you get home from work or if there's going to be a show-down over something trivial."

"It depends. Sometimes I'm fed up and you're the nearest thing to take out my frustrations on. Sorry. That's what marriage is about, isn't it?"

"No it jolly well isn't," spluttered Norma. "How can you suddenly come out with that? You were so kind and considerate until about six months ago."

"That's what you think. I don't think the kids will say that."

"You mean you've been hurting them?"

"Better ask them, hadn't you?"

"You bet I will! Things are going to have to change here, I've had enough!"

They discussed the problems that they were facing. James felt that Norma favoured the children above him and couldn't help resenting them.

It was decided that James should move out of the home and Norma would find a position in another firm, while they prepared for divorce. Norma's girls later told her that James had frequently hit them and they accused their mother of not stopping his abuse. They felt that she should have been aware and suspicious of their step-father's behaviour. James had always been very careful to administer his punishments and threats when Norma was out.

How was she to know? she wondered when she was alone. No one had told her and she was not clairvoyant. She knew that she could only continue to do her best for the children, even if they could not appreciate it.

It was a very fraught time for the family, but Norma was able to secure the home, which she had so lovingly fostered for them so that they would not be homeless.

The 'right to buy' legislation in 1980, under Mrs. Thatcher's government had given council house tenants the opportunity of purchase, so with the money that she received from the divorce, Norma was able to buy her own home. She decided to change its configuration and had walls removed in order to make a through lounge/diner, had the position of the lounge door turned so the entrance hall gained character and treated herself to a new kitchen.

The children grew up safely in a calmer atmosphere with their mother, whilst their grandparents, particularly Amy, despite her illness, gave as much support as possible to the family.

To Norma's horror, two years after her divorce she read in the local newspaper, of the death of her former husband. At the age of forty, his life was over as he had suffered the agonies of stomach cancer. Perhaps this illness had changed his disposition, or perhaps it was just familiarity and contempt that had made him become violent. After his death, his sister said that he had been a destructive child, but had grown out of the temper tantrums and anti-social behaviour as far as she knew. Had he been in pain? He probably felt dreadful a lot of the time during his final years of life, but why had he not told her? Thoughts tumbled like a washing machine around in Norma's head, but she knew it would have been self harming had she allowed the marriage to continue; and would have probably put her children's lives in danger.

By the time Norma attended James' funeral with her mother, she had few tears that she could shed for the man in whom she had once so lovingly put her trust. She promised herself that from then onwards she was better off without a man in her life.

At the age of eighteen Alex joined the 2nd Paras. He loved the Army until he had fought at Goose Green in the Falklands War of 1982. He was mentioned in dispatches, as he had been the bodyguard of Lieutenant—Colonel Herbert 'H' Jones, who was one of the men who was so tragically killed, along with many of his colleagues. He never recovered from this ordeal and left the Army two years after. He emigrated to North America in order to start a new life in 1988, only revisiting England on occasion; a fact that Norma had difficulty in accepting. He was her first born and very like his father, who often filled her thoughts.

Alice was a conscientious student at school and gained sufficient GCSEs to attend the college of Further Education to study Art. She later became a Graphic Designer with a firm in London.

Andrina remained demanding of her mother's time and energy. She studied secretarial work and became a PA to a company director, whom she later married when she was twenty years old.

Norma threw herself into her work and in 1984, had become the Office Manager in the firm. She was able to put her creative talent to good use when she chose suitable décor for the meeting rooms and offices.
Norma enjoyed life to the full. She bought herself a racy sports car, enjoyed the occasional nights out with her girlfriends and lived vicariously through her children's lives.

With the children flown the nest, Norma gave up the job which had given her the money and stability, necessary to bring up a growing family, and became a member of a caring team. Her new job was to help drug addicts and inadequate people through their difficulties. This often involved staying over in their houses whilst refurbishing their homes through paper-hanging, painting, making matching furnishings, or recovering chairs and settees that had seen better days. Norma loved bringing her talents to this job and was content to know that she was helping others who were less fortunate than herself. Who better than someone who had known hard times themselves?

Norma made good friends amongst her colleagues, who were a constant support for her and she was often to be found in the local bar with a glass in her hand, chatting easily to anyone and everyone. She was a free agent now that her parental responsibilities were over and she was determined to enjoy herself.

At the age of forty-eight Norma met George Jackson who ran his own driving school. The children were all safely married, with children of their own, whom she saw occasionally. George offered her a social life and security in her old age, so she agreed to a marriage. Her parents were delighted to see her happy again; for, indeed she was. She refused to take any notice of the teasing of marrying someone with her maiden name. As she pointed out, she had been Hill in between and she had managed that without any trouble.

George knew how to wine and dine her and they went out to dinner every Friday night. They both loved the sun, so went on cruises to the Greek Islands and around the Mediterranean. Although Norma did not have the same intensity of feelings for George as she had experienced with Alexis, she realised that teenage love was very different from that of a middle-aged woman. Both families gelled and all the children were friends, which was a blessing for family occasions. Her cooking prowess proved to be a subject to break the ice at these events. She was frequently thankful for the training given by her mother in her very early years. She had developed a real joy for cooking meals and cakes for others. Life was good.

The only drawback to the marriage was that George was feckless with money and they often found themselves in debt. George's attitude to money had been a concern of hers for years. This irked Norma who had always kept a strict hold on finances when she was on her own. She had always shielded the children from difficult times when they had been without a man's wage to help with the running costs. Her priorities had been to provide a meal, clothes and warmth for her children, unlike his irresponsible approach towards finance.

They began to row and their relationship suffered. Although Norma loved him, the marriage was threatened when she found a huge lorry outside the house on her return from work one day.

"Whoever has parked that in front of the house?" she asked her husband who was sitting on the sofa drinking a cup of tea.

"Would you like a cuppa?" he asked sweetly.

"Come on, George. What is it?" demanded Norma.

"Well . . ."

"Yes."

"It was such a good deal."

"What! It's yours?" Norma asked disbelievingly.

"Only 8,000."

"But we don't have 8,000."

"We'll soon get it back."

"And how do you intend doing that? You don't have a heavy goods licence . . . or do you?"

"No. but I can employ a driver."

"Yes, you can; to drive this monstrosity away. Preferably back to the bloke who sold it to you and you can ask for your money back."

"Can't do that . . . It was a good deal, Norma . . . I'll make it work."

Norma paused. Was it worth arguing and making herself ill, because that was how she felt when they argued? She decided that enough was enough.

"OK. If that's how you feel, you can make it work somewhere else. I'm NOT having a lorry parked outside my house."

Despite his pleading nothing would change Norma's mind. It was a residential area and most people had bought their houses so wanted to make a good home for themselves. She was not prepared to make life unpleasant for her neighbours.

"We must stay together. We love each other," George pleaded. "I can't get rid of the lorry, but I won't do anything as stupid again."

"You will. You always do. I can't cope with the debts any more. I need to manage my own money and not be beholden to you in any way. You need to be gone by the weekend."

Norma was exasperated with him. She knew it was like a disease for him. He loved a good time—and had included her in all their social outings—but she hated not knowing where the next meal would come from or whether a cheque would bounce. She knew that they had a good relationship and she did not want to lose that. It was years since the love of her life had deserted her and she needed someone to care, so she came up with a compromise.

"We'll still see each other and go out together, but you can't live here. We'll have our own monies and bank accounts, so will be independent of each other financially. That's the only way it'll work, George. Will you try it out for a few months, eh?" Norma pleaded.

"I'll think about it," he replied.

"YOU ALWAYS SAY THAT," she screamed at him. "IT'S TOO LATE FOR THINKING. YES OR NO?"

"OK," George replied, "don't get so worked up."

"WORKED UP, IS IT? YOU HAVE NO IDEA WHAT YOU ARE PUTTING ME THROUGH, HAVE YOU? YOU CAN PACK YOUR BAGS NOW. ON SECOND THOUGHTS I'LL DO THEM FOR YOU."

Norma stormed out of the room and flew up the stairs into their bedroom. She threw open a case and bundled George's clothes into the space. Then she took his books off the shelves and made a pile of them. She looked around. There were not a lot of possessions that were his and his alone. She began to calm down, but forced herself to keep her resolve.

She struggled down the stairs and said,

"There you are. You can drive off into the sunset. Have you phoned someone to fetch the lorry?"

George could see that he was defeated.

"Yes. It's all in hand. My daughter says I can have a room at their house until I can get something of my own."

He walked across the carpet towards her and stretched out his arms.

"Don't!" Norma said.

She was on the verge of tears and did not want the effect of his going to be affected by these wretched droplets that always accompanied a row. If only her feelings could stay on an even keel, but she knew that this would rarely be the case.

George eventually left their home, but both still remained faithful to each other and they could often be seen enjoying the night life and experiencing wonderful holidays together.

However, tragedy followed Norma around like a stalker. Within thirteen years, both her parents had died and George was diagnosed with cancer.

Norma gave up her job and George returned to the house so that she could become his carer. Although she could have booked him into the local Hospice, she decided to nurse him herself with help from MacMillan Nurses. As he died in her arms, he apologised for not showing her how much he had loved her. She thought her heart would break. It was going to take years for her to recover.

She now had only her home that she had created and three successful children, although her relationship with them was turbulent. Norma knew that she would have to work for the rest of her life if she was going to remain sane. She needed to be occupied so that she did not think about her past.

Hopefully, as she was now of pensionable age, Norma would find some respite from the problems that had followed her around.

A new development in an adjoining village had just been completed and there were advertisements for cleaners of the larger Town Houses. Norma decided that there would be few demands on her if she was able to secure such a position and the extra money would supplement her pension. Her friends thought she was selling herself too cheaply, but Norma knew that this job would suffice.

She started her new work within a week and was happy to clean up for the rich people who abused their beautiful houses. Most of them, however, were appreciative and Christmas meant a number of bottles of wine and boxes of chocolates, which could be shared with the family.
With a busy and tiring life again, Norma began the slow healing process.

Chapter 18   Changes

Joanna and Julian struggled along through almost twenty years of being tied 'Til death do us part'. Neither of them found enough stimulation in the marriage and sought other things to fulfil their needs.
Julian became obsessed with being 'in charge' and took a position in a small firm that regarded him as the boss' deputy. He also became the Chairperson of the village Community Centre. He insisted in attending every sub committee meeting, which ensured that he was out of the home for at least one evening every week. He had put aside a further evening for meeting the lorry drivers in the firm and this developed into *another* evening when he met socially with the transport manager.

But, when Julian began to be away from home overnight twice a week, Joanna wondered if he was having an affair. He kept a case ready packed for these occasions, collecting it whilst Joanna was at work. He always left a note: 'Will phone you to make sure that Sophie is alright. Will be back tomorrow night, unless something unforeseen crops up.' At one time he signed off with love and a kiss, but that rarely appeared towards the end of the marriage.

Rows became frequent, although Julian was careful to imply that it was Joanna's fault if ever Sophie was in earshot, which was a ploy that he had always used.

Steven gained more qualifications and came home only monthly—to make sure his mother could organise his washing and his life that he found hard to come to terms with. He coped well considering his poor start, but the world is a harsh desert if you do not know your background and have been forced to rely on Houseparents in Children's Homes in your young life. Joanna was glad that she and Julian had provided him with a home.

Steven's conversation and concern for her well being did not mirror her husband's attitude, which was increasingly indifferent. Joanna looked forward to her son's visits home and a chance for adult conversation. Her colleagues had been kind and understanding, but they had no knowledge of the problems that there were in the home. Joanna knew that Steven appreciated the difficulties even if they were not expressed in words. Julian had often found him a trial, but she had managed to keep the peace between them and their relationship had improved since Steven had moved on, although they had bonded closely during their Rugby years together. Once Julian had been forced to give up on his beloved Rugby playing, he had trained the Colts team at the club in Essex, at which Steven had made his mark as a Prop Forward.

Sophie adored her 'big brother' and they could often be found in close conversation. Joanna thought of the times that they had watched 'Lassie' on the television. Sophie would be sat on Steven's expansive knee, cuddled into his chest, whilst huge tears rolled down the faces of both as they saw Lassie's dice with death or her remarkable attempts at finding her lost owners again. They had developed a bond that made Joanna's heart sing; they truly loved each other. Sophie had not known life without Steven and he had unreservedly taken her on as his little sister, protecting her from the evils of a world that he had already experienced.

She felt truly blessed with her children.

Extracts from Joanna's diary

December 1980
I don't really think I care any more. How could he make such a fuss over the cooking of the turkey? Spoiling Christmas day for everyone as usual. Said I'd cooked it the wrong way up . . . Don't you turn turkeys? Xpect it's 'cause I said he couldn't plant his beans on Boxing Day . . . not with Mum & Dad here. He's a REAL B****** Good job Steve is in Scotland—at least he didn't have to witness the outburst. Poor little Sophie; Mum was wonderful with her.

February 1981
Sophie feels that she never sees anything of her Daddy. I mentioned this to him so HE WENT AND BOUGHT TIGERS SEASON TICKETS for them both . . . for a nine year old girl!? Will have to get knitting! Steven

very pleased as this means he can cash in on the deal and come home to watch class rugby sometimes, when he isn't playing for The Beavers Ist. Team—which won't be often—but it's made him happy!
Julian made Church Warden. HA HA. He's a REAL ICON TO EMULATE!!

March 15th.
His birthday. Wanted sex. Ripped nightie apart from neck to toe. Forced himself on to me. Really frightened. Have knitted Sophie all the gear for rugby-leg warmers, hat, scarf and gloves; she looks lovely. It seems to have brought her and dad closer together.
Mum and Dad came to my cousin's silver wedding do. They are going abroad to celebrate so we decided to give them a dinner party as our present to them.

March 17th.
In the night after the silver wedding party, I heard my parents in the bathroom. Mum felt very ill, so I phoned for the doctor. He came three hours later! Said she had obviously eaten something that hadn't agreed with her. Dad stayed with Mum all morning, but was worried and said he felt there was something drastically wrong. Sent for another doctor yesterday; he came within half an hour. He phoned for the ambulance. Mum said, "Make them take me. I'm shaking and can't last much longer." Dad and I followed in the car, after I had taken Sophie to her friend's house. By the time we got to the Hospital, Mum was in the CCU because she had had a heart attack.
Dad is devastated. So am I.

March19th
Visiting Mum every evening or afternoon. Looking awful. Doesn't want them to keep trying to keep her alive. Dad spoke to doctor, but he said that it was his job to keep her alive and not to let her die. All very upsetting. We all hate this waiting.

April 2nd.
Mum being moved to rehab tomorrow. She wants me to look for a small house near us—she has noticed some at the top of the rise.

April 10th
Had a phone call on 3rd. Mum died in the ambulance en route to the rehab place in Quorn. Felt SO numb. Dad being very brave. Says she would

have been a cabbage if she'd lived. Had a lot wrong with her I suppose.
He told me that he was glad they had adopted me; never remarked on
this before, bless him. Funeral was yesterday at the Crem. No one from
Stamford came—just the family. Had lots of letters and expect Dad will
have some when he goes home.

May 1981.
Dad decided to go back to Stamford at end of April. He looked very
forlorn. Says the dog will keep him going. Beginning to feel very low.
Don't think I grieved enough as trying to keep Dad going. Julian
HOPELESS. Doesn't seem to have any empathy and certainly isn't
interested in my grief. At least the children know how I'm feeling, thank
goodness.

June 1981
Had to listen to how he had a hostess for the evening at a London 'do'.
What does it really mean?
Feeling very down. Can't get through the Lord's Prayer in church without
crying. Have had to leave four times already. Julian tells me to pull myself
together. Just can't. Sophie lovely. Knows I need a lot of cuddles. She and
Steve know how to behave in these situations—Julian seems to be at sea;
perhaps he's better with people he doesn't know well!!!!!!

September 1981
Another frightening night. When I told him that if you force sex on
someone who doesn't want it he replied that a husband cannot rape a
wife, so needn't try to go to anyone. Daren't tell anyone so don't know if
he's right or not. Life's unbearable. Thank god I've got the children.

Patrick's dog became ill, so he asked Joanna if he could
bring him over so that Julian could take him to the vet.

"If he has to be put down, let it be," were the words he said
as Julian took the old boy off in the car.

Patrick sobbed.

"That's two then," he said cryptically.

That night, when Sophie was in bed and the three of them
were seated in the living room, Patrick asked,

"What would your mother have decided to do if I had gone first?"

"Oh, she had envisaged living in a little house up the road near to us."

"Um. I don't think I can manage on my own now, especially now the dog's gone. That's two in Leicester, so I should make the third."

Joanna suddenly realised that her perky, phlegmatic father had aged beyond all reason.

There was a silence, which Julian, as usual filled.

"OK. We'll get Doug, our builder friend, to draw up some plans and perhaps we can have an extension on the house," he suggested.

"That would be great, wouldn't it Dad?"

"Yes. I think so."

"We'll get Doug to come round whilst you're here and you can go back to Stamford knowing what it entails."

A Grand-dad flat was built and Patrick moved in within the year.

By January 1982, Julian was staying out for an extra night when he went away on business, because 'something has cropped up', so Joanna became suspicious. When she confronted him, Julian assured her that he was not involved with a woman, but she continued to question his movements. Eventually he snapped.

"If you must know, I can't bear being with you. In four years time, we shall review our marriage and then we'll take it from there. O.K?"

No wonder he hardly came to bed with her at night, or got up before she awoke; he obviously could not stand her. Joanna felt devastated. She had not gone into marriage expecting it to fail and though she had worked hard at preserving this state, she was horrified to hear her husband say these words.

Sophie was now 10.

Extract from Joanna's diary

April 1982
"I love you but don't like you" is the latest mantra. WHAT?! He says he goes to church to get him through life and that he HAS to repent. I said he didn't behave any better from Monday to Sunday. It's MY FAULT apparently.
He is beginning to drink heavily . . . because he lives with me. Of course! What am I going to do?
Have been asked to play the organ at church as Bertha is getting too old. Not very confident, but Julian says I have no choice and I should get on with it.
Dad thinks it is a wonderful opportunity!

September 1982
Another night away at a Dinner. Had the same hostess whose name, he says, is Joanna. He tells me it makes it easier for him—in case he shouts out her name in his sleep. What a SH**. Rarely sleep together now. He never comes to bed with me and is not there when I wake up so don't know what he does. Where did I go wrong???

Joanna decided that she should develop her career and she applied and was accepted on a course that gave her an Advanced Diploma in Education and Management at the University of Leicester.

Julian had not been very co-operative about this venture, but recognised that it could mean a promotion for his wife. That would mean financial benefits for him, but it also meant that he had to take some responsibility for his daughter when Joanna was at the University every Monday and Wednesday evening. He was able to take the opportunity to bond with Sophie and they would be able to discuss the match that they had seen on the previous Saturday during the Rugby season. Anyway, he had no quarrel with Sophie; she was like his side of the family so she was easy to love.

When Julian was too late home for comfort, Patrick happily 'baby-sat' his grand-daughter. He loved her company and like most young people, her grandfather was special to her. Steven also enjoyed seeing 'the old boy'—although he had been closer to Pamela when he had first come onto the scene. He was aware that they had been very supportive of him and his situation. Pamela had told him how she and her husband had adopted his new mother and how much joy she had brought them.

March 1983
Julian must sometimes sleep in Steve's room as have been presented with those sheets for washing. When I asked if this is an indication of the end he asked me what I thought. To the world he presents as a considerate and caring husband and father. Sophie says I let him bully me and I should stand up to him. Not prepared to tell her what he might do to me. Enjoying the course and it has given me more insight into the learning process. No wonder the kids with problems don't like school. Try to make it bearable for them when they are in the class. Wish it could do something about my faith-how can God let me endure this amount of crap? Julian presents as a wonderful human being to the world and my father, but I see the true man. Is his behaviour towards me that of a Christian?

Whilst Joanna was doing her course, she met a woman of her own age who was about to join The Special Educational Needs Service. This was a newly developed service in Leicestershire in preparation for the 1984 Education Act. She talked to Julian about joining the service; he advised her to discuss this prospect with her Headteacher, who urged her:

"Go for it Joanna. You'll be good."

Joanna knew that the head would be relieved if she moved on as they did not often agree over his 'over diplomatic' approach to issues within the school.

Sophie and her mother left the Primary School where they had blossomed. There were many flowers and boxes of chocolates bestowed on Joanna from grateful parents and Sophie came away with gifts from classmates who were going on to other schools. The summer holidays were spent in anticipation of a huge change to their lives. Julian took them away on a trip to Europe, which was a wonderful experience for Sophie, but torture for Joanna as her husband blamed her for every problem that they encountered.

On the morning that an anxious Sophie went to the local Secondary School on the school bus, her mother drove her car to the HQ of the Special Needs Service to embark on a 'new' career.

CHAPTER 19   Conquering Times

Joanna had been appointed to the Special Educational Needs team in Leicestershire and was based at a school in the county. Initially, she worked only in her base school and spent a lot of time on the phone setting up meetings with Heads to inform them of what the new service could offer. She also met and assessed pupils at the base school and gradually her work took her further afield. Julian had little interest in Joanna's career and they rarely discussed their daily events.

Joanna threw herself into her new role. She became well respected in the area in which she worked as a Learning Difficulties Tutor and gained sufficient kudos to sustain her ego.

Unwittingly, on her visits to other schools, Joanna started to look at other couples and their relationships. She even began to look at available men and wonder what they would be like to be with. She had not intended to fall for anyone, but eventually, Joanna had to surrender everything when she met her soul mate at work in 1984.

Extract from Joanna's diary

November 1984
Love my new job and have a good room at my base; a really nice school and very welcoming to me. Met a nice guy who needed to use the phone in my office. Seemed shy. His voice was as deep as that of Vincent Price.

Joanna wondered if her heart-beat could be heard by a hard of hearing passer by. This man was lovely, a bit like Dennis Waterman, who was her 'heart throb' on the television. She knew she would have to find out who he was.

When she went down to the Staff Room at lunch time, she found the DW look-alike talking with a teacher she already supported in the classroom.
"Do you know Hugh?"

"Oh. Hello. We met in my office," she replied, feeling a flush spread over her face. (Why did she always have to blush in such circumstances?)

"Perhaps you could help me in the classroom?"

"I expect so, but you'll have to see Ian; he designs my time table in this school. What do you teach?"

"History."

"Oh, good. I like the subject. Did it for A level."

"Great. Well, must get back."

With this, Hugh turned and scuttled off.

"Is he shy, or something?" asked Joanna.

"Just getting over a divorce," was the reply.

Joanna's thoughts whirled. Divorce.

Now there was something she had not considered where Julian was concerned. He was hinting that life with her was unbearable and she felt the same about living with him. But what about Sophie? And Steven would probably not be too chuffed either, although he was a grown man and would soon have girlfriends—she hoped.

One break, Joanna found Hugh talking to a pretty blonde girl in the Staff Room. Joanna felt a stab of jealousy as they seemed so relaxed with each other. The Blonde had been on a term's secondment in France. Suddenly Joanna heard her ask, "How's Sophie?"

At the first available opportunity Joanna joined the conversation.

"My daughter's name is Sophie too."

This broke the ice and Hugh and Joanna started to talk about their little girls. It was quite amazing; neither Hugh nor Joanna had chosen the name, although they had both chosen Jonathan as the boy's name had a son been born to them.

Hugh began to fill Joanna's thoughts and she found herself looking for him. He had written a musical that was being performed by the school. As it was on Sophie's birthday, Joanna apologised to him for being unable to attend but wishing him luck. Hugh was impressed that she had bothered to say anything; she was a nice woman, as everyone had told him.

Hugh rarely joined a group who went out on a Friday lunchtime, but one day he suggested they walk along together when they found themselves leaving the premises at the same time. As they walked along they chatted about literature and music, although she hardly knew any of the artists that he mentioned.

Next term, Joanna found that she had been allocated four lessons of History with Hugh. He was an amazing teacher, who brought his subject to life, with a good balance of humour and discipline, being both firm but kind to his pupils. He was well liked and the pupils were spell bound by his knowledge, as was Joanna. In conversation, she discovered that he had a double honours in English and History.
Not only good looking, but clever too, she thought!

January 1985
Have been given pupils to support in Hugh's class. He's a gifted teacher and ready to accept ideas for helping the less able pupils access his work. HE was out again: only has Sundays at home these days. S comes home some weekends and they all go to Tigers. At least I get a chance to stock up the freezer for the week's meals.
The whisky is flowing big time. I try to keep out of the way as it's only abuse thrown at me. I am now 'a f****** cow'. Am SO unhappy and frustrated. At least separate rooms mean he can't rape me any more.

Joanna realised that she was looking forward to supporting Hugh and the pupils with learning difficulties in his classes. She revamped worksheets to make them accessible and more enjoyable for the slower learner and made suggestions about Hugh's classroom displays. He took everything on board.

Hugh felt that he was beginning to live again after his horrendous ten years of marriage. Joanna felt that she was being valued for herself as well as having someone interested in what she had to offer through her career.

May 1985
Hugh and I are the only teachers who don't live in the town so can't go home for lunch whilst we are on strike. We both go into town. Have had coffee two or three times.
Head asked if I could go on a school trip with Hugh as the original teacher has to be back for his stag night! I said I would as long as I can take Sophie. Hugh is taking his little daughter.

June 1985
Had a super day in York. Trip went well. Falling for Hugh! Hmm . . .

As Julian was so busy with work or at meetings, it fell to Joanna to act as the taxi service for her daughter. Sophie had taken to doing homework with her 'best friend' who lived round the corner, but she needed to be collected every evening at 8pm.

It was decided by the Service, for whom Joanna worked, that all personnel should have a qualification in Special Educational Needs. As Joanna had attained her Advanced Diploma there, Leicester University was again pleased to offer her a course in order for her gain an SEN Certificate. Julian was forced to become involved with his daughter's collection on the night that Joanna was studying. He had to walk, which did not please him, because Joanna had the car in order to get to Leicester. Grand-dad was always on hand if necessary, but Joanna was not keen for him to be out in the cold night air.

Sophie often sided with her mother when Julian was being difficult. She once was so angry with her father over him picking a fight with her mother that she snapped,

"Leave Mummy alone. She doesn't sit down once she's home from school. She makes our tea and then frets about yours getting spoiled when you don't get home on time. Then all you do is read the paper. We wash up and clear away whilst you do nothing. My Mummy works hard too. It's not just you."

She had stormed off to her room and Julian had gone up to her. Of course, it had ended in tears and Sophie had been too distressed to complete her homework, so Joanna had to write a letter to the teacher and explain that Sophie had been unwell and unable to complete her work.

Joanna began to have problems with her hands and feet. The Hospital told her that she had arthritis and there was little that could be done except for taking pain killers. One day, she was in the Staff Room and was telling a colleague that driving was becoming increasingly difficult for her because of the condition. Hugh joined in the conversation.

"I know a really good bloke in Coventry, who treated my daughter for a skin complaint. He's an iridologist and herbalist and VERY good."

"Oh anything, quite honestly. What is an iridologist?"

Hugh explained and added, "I'll ask my ex for his number so that you can make an appointment."

"Oh, thanks. That's really kind, Hugh."

Joanna did not expect anything to come of the conversation, but when she next supported Hugh in the classroom, he gave her the name and phone number of the iridologist. Joanna made the appointment and Hugh offered to take her to the clinic for treatment. He told her to bring her daughter along because he would have his, as it was his turn to have her to sleep over at the weekend.

Sophie accompanied her mother on all the excursions to Coventry. Joanna had her treatment and Sophie went round the shops for the hour with Hugh and his daughter. They also went to Leamington, where Hugh had a flat, when the schools were on strike. His daughter was always there as well and the girls became increasingly jealous of each other, although seemed to enjoy the activities that were offered by their parents. Pizza Express was a favourite for the girls and

Joanna was pleased to be able to pay. She knew that Hugh had little money to spare and had even bought some curtains for him.

"Your little girl will be cold as Winter approaches unless you have curtains. Would you like to choose some from my catalogue? You can pay monthly and then it won't be too difficult for you."

"OK. That looks a good deal. Thanks."

Hugh made a tape for Joanna of all the songs that he thought she might like. Among them were: 'The River' by Bruce Springsteen, Dan Hill's 'Sometimes when we touch', 'Smile' by Eric Clapton and Gordon Lightfoot's 'If you could read my mind'. He left it in her pigeon hole in the Staff Room. She listened to it repeatedly and began to wonder if the words were a message to her.

During the Summer holidays, Joanna and Sophie received a postcard from 'Hugh and Sophie'. Julian demanded to know who they were, but Sophie intervened.

"Hugh's a teacher at Mummy's school and Sophie is his daughter. They're ever so nice and we have outings together, don't we, Mum?"

"Yes dear, we do." She looked at her husband who raised an enquiring eyebrow. "There's nothing 'untoward' happening, Julian. We are just befriending a lonely colleague who is going through a difficult time."

"Well you just make sure that it stays that way," growled Julian.

"Of course," smiled Joanna, hoping that he could not hear her heart, which seemed to be beating very hard against her ribs. After all, she and Hugh were not romantically involved and she was only doing her Christian duty. Wasn't she?

Julian soon became bored with such talk and he prepared to go into the room to read the paper.

Joanna started to make an additional pie or put aside some eggs, which she surreptitiously slipped into Hugh's unlocked car, whenever the opportunity arose. Her maternal instinct responded to his pale, lean appearance.

They increasingly found themselves drawn to each other during free periods. They discovered they had a lot in common and enjoyed discussing their experiences of music and theatre.

November 1985
Another strike. Sophie with her friend for day so went over to Hugh's.
One thing led to another and we found ourselves in bed together. Told him
about rapes etc. He said I could always go and live with him! He was quite
wonderful. I think he loves me too.
Tentatively suggested to Sophie that we could be leaving. She said she
wanted to stay because of her best friend and her boyfriend. Said that as
long I saw her every week, she'd be O.K. She guessed it was Hugh...

Joanna looked in her pigeon hole in the Staff Room. There was a little white business card of her Herbalist and on the back, a message: 'Tree climbing rodents?'

This was an invitation to go to The Common and share sandwiches with Hugh during the lunch hour. Perhaps he was as much in love with her, as she was with him, she thought. Joanna's heart sang, her eyes sparkled and she felt happier than she had been since childhood. She now felt less afraid of Julian than she had ever done. If he found out that she was in love with someone else, there would be repercussions. But she did not care about him any more. Steven and Sophie would be OK because they knew how awful Julian could be. His nastiness had even caused the caretaker at her previous school to make the comment, 'A right little Hitler he is. How can you bear him?'; so Joanna knew she was not imagining it.

Hugh was kind, considerate, caring, gentle, understanding and not at all like the self-righteous man she was married to. Hugh was also amusing and made her laugh; a good recipe for happiness.

Towards the end of term Joanna and Hugh celebrated an early Christmas with an Indian take-away. They exchanged presents. As Hugh did not want Julian to find his gift of love, he had purchased a special mug for Joanna to use at school. Joanna had given Hugh a gift voucher for clothes and the latest Lloyd Cole LP.

"It will be a long time before we can be together, but I love you."

"I love you too," replied Joanna, snuggling into the embrace of her lover.

Little did they realise that time goes quickly when you are enjoying yourself and that real time catches up eventually.

Julian sensed that there was a man in Joanna's life because she was too happy; he decided to join her in bed just after New Year. He was angry when she told him that she would not let him near her.

"You haven't wanted me for over 18 months. Don't expect to come back now."

"Yes . . . You have a man. Is it that herbalist bloke?" he demanded, stabbing an accusing finger at her.

"You've not seen him. Otherwise you'd know he had nothing but his skills to recommend him!"

"Who is it then?" Julian sneered.

For the first time since she had known him, Joanna was not afraid of him or what he might do.

"It's Hugh. From school."

Julian paused, took a deep breath and declared,

"Right. You can go. I don't want you. We'll have the Priest round tomorrow first thing."

Joanna could hear him in the bathroom. He had always vomited when he was nervous or distressed, so she let him get on with his discomfiture. She felt that he had made her suffer for too long for her to show much compassion. She went to the phone and rang Hugh's number.

"He knows."

"Oh. Well you know you can come here, don't you? Don't worry. I love you."

"I love you too."

Suddenly she felt guilty. She went upstairs.

"Can I get you anything?" she whispered through the bathroom door.

"Yes. Get out of my life, you bloody cow."

He had always resorted to bad language or abusive comments when he was irritated with her, so she did not blanche at his words and they no longer hurt her. In fact, this time he was the one hurt, which gave Joanna some satisfaction.

Neither of them slept. Joanna was already dressed when she heard her husband make the call to their Parish Priest.

When he arrived at eight thirty, the conversation was one-sided. Joanna felt absolute hatred for Julian. Eventually she turned to their friend in robes,

"I don't know why, but I can't bear Julian. He destroyed our marriage years ago."

"How dare you say such a thing? I'm not the one who's committed adultery."

Joanna knew that it was impossible to argue her corner and she was saved any more embarrassment by the words,

"I think the marriage is dead, Julian. I can't see how you can mend this. It's too late. You know where I am when you need me."

Julian suggested that Joanna went to pack and then say goodbye to her father whilst he organised what to do with

Sophie. Joanna insisted that she tell her daughter and held her in her arms.

"Don't worry, Mummy. I'll still see you and I can manage with Nat and Leeco. Daddy and I can go to Rugby and I can do the meals."
It broke Joanna's heart.

"I haven't stopped loving you. I can't help not loving Daddy. He doesn't love me either, you know."

"Oh. Steve told me that ages ago. It's obvious anyway. I expect you stayed together because I was young. Parents do that. There's lots at school."

The knowledge and worldliness of youth is staggering to parents.
Julian was not as sanguine. He had wanted to be the one to end the marriage in a year's time; he had wanted to keep the upper hand and he had wanted to decide how their lives could be shown to the world. Instead, this 'dreadful woman' had messed up all his plans. He decided to make sure that she would suffer.

Firstly, Julian demanded that she leave the marital home by the afternoon and have limited contact with her daughter. Steven had already left home, but Julian felt sure he could force him to reject his foster mother. He had always been able to frighten him into submission with threats, and saw no reason why this should not continue to work.

Secondly, he would work towards their children having no contact with her. He knew that if the boot had been on the other foot, she would not have played it this way, but he wanted to destroy her.

Thirdly, he could turn the state of affairs round to his advantage and no-one need know that he had intended to leave when Sophie was sixteen. Anyone who wanted to continue a friendship with his 'adulterous wife' should not expect any contact with the children or him. He loathed her as much as she now loathed him and he wanted others

172

to loathe her too. There was to be no compromise on friendships, it was either him or her.

He promised her that he *knew* what he would do and she would eventually pay for this embarrassing situation. Funny how people see break-ups differently. Joanna surrendered a lot, because she chose love before duty and that was unheard of in the family.

She packed her suitcase, gathered her treasures together and prepared to leave. Her father was appalled at the little she was taking.

"You can't go with only that amount of stuff. You'll need bedding and pots and pans."

"Don't fuss, grand-dad. She can make two journeys today and I'll get a box together for when she comes back on Monday to see you," said Julian.

He was anxious to get Joanna away so that he could go round to Sophie's friend's house and then phone his mate in Derby. He'd come down and help him through this difficult patch.

Joanna drove away from her well appointed detached house and sped towards her soul-mate in his two bedroom flat in Warwickshire.

When she arrived, she let herself into the flat with the key that she had been given only two weeks earlier. Hugh was not there. She put the case and boxes in the hall and got back into her car.

It occurred to her that she was taking a big risk. She and Hugh had only been alone together on five occasions. Both of them had been starved of physical love for years, which was probably why their unions were so wonderful.

Could she be jumping from the frying pan into the fire? Perhaps she was only another notch in Hugh's belt, or a play—thing to satisfy his needs and he would drop her when he was finished with her. She would fall from a great height! In her heart she knew Hugh wouldn't let her down.

Whatever life held for her, Joanna knew that it would be better than being with Julian, to whom she would never return.

Leaving her precious Sophie was a huge wrench and she prayed that Julian would not be too difficult and manipulating over contact with her daughter. She felt sure that Steven would be O.K. when he heard. He had known what his father was like. When Steven was still living at home he had experienced the erratic moods and constrained atmosphere; it had often been necessary to walk on eggshells.

As Joanna packed the car for a second time with sheets and a duvet—which she later learned was her father's doing—two pots, a salad bowl, a sugar bowl that had been her grandmother's, and a fruit bowl that had been a Christmas present from Joan, she knew that she had little to show for almost twenty years of marriage. Hugh knew that he had a damaged ego to heal.

Chapter 20   Life After Heartache

Hugh was amazed to hear a little voice from behind his
driving seat exclaim,

"Look! There's Joanna's car."

He had taken his ex wife and their little daughter on a
picnic because it had been an unexpectedly glorious day
for January. As soon as he arrived back at their house, he
phoned his own number and willed Joanna to pick up.

"I'll be home in a second. Are you OK?"

She had felt quite calm but as soon as Hugh spoke so lovingly
to her, the tears began to flow.

"I'm on my way," he said reassuringly.

Within a few hours they felt that they had always lived
together. It was quite remarkable. Joanna knew that they
'had been made for each other', as her mother would have
said. How glad she would have been to know her new man
and to see her so happy!

Extracts from Joanna's diary

January 20th 1986
*HE wants a meeting. Hugh says it has to be at the house, NOT in a pub
car park as requested.*

Julian demanded that Joanna sign over the house. In a
belligerent and bitter meeting they decided that she could
leave the marriage with the knowledge that she would have
£5,500, plus the car. Although Joanna realized that this was
a ridiculously poor remuneration for almost twenty years of
marriage, she could not bear the small-minded demands of
the man who had once been her husband. Her main priority
was to be free of her unhappy past.

The passion she had found in her new relationship was
as intense as that experienced by her birth mother and

father (although she obviously did not know this) and she was determined that nothing could destroy her new found happiness.

Extracts from Joanna's diary

January 21st
I know that I've given up everything—a detached house, money, an inheritance which I would have had from Joan; after the letter I have had, I doubt I shall receive anything. She says I'm selfish etc. etc. : she has NO idea how awful life has been with J) It will all be worth it. I KNOW WE SHALL BE ALRIGHT. ALL FOR LOVE. NOTHING WILL MAKE ME RETURN—NOT EVEN SOPHIE.

24th.
Saw Dad before I went into the main house. He told me to be careful. He would stand in the kitchen so that he could be on hand if necessary. Wonder what he has done or said to Dad? J. wants me to go back—for Sophie's sake. Told him I couldn't do so and that I loathe him—imagine what he'd be like now. I shall see Sophie regularly and she knows she can come and live with us if life becomes unbearable for her. HE was frightful. He's lost the upper-hand and therefore, CONTROL.
But, I insisted that he cashed in some annuities, which my money bought, but agreed to let him have the house. Says I can have the car—especially as I paid for it each month!
Know I'm losing out; he didn't offer anything except £5,500 (car plus cashed in annuities) but at least I'm happy. Just wish Sophie could understand and be a bit more supportive. Perhaps he's being awkward.

Joanna went to the house on three evenings of the week, whilst Hugh taught at Night School. On one evening, she took Sophie out and spent the other two seeing both her father and Sophie. Julian decided that Joanna could pay maintenance, rather than treat her to meals each week. Joanna agreed to give money, but insisted that it went through the courts.

But Julian had another trick up his sleeve.

All the documentation went through without too much difficulty and three weeks after signing over the house in March, Joanna had a note to tell her that Sophie no longer wanted to see her.

Extracts from Joanna's diary.

March 1986
Devastated. Wrote to Sophie enclosing money. Expect she's being poisoned against me. At least I know that I never told her what he was like to me. When I tried, she said it was my fault for letting him treat me so badly.

May 1986
Sophie has forgotten all the running about that I did for her. Has refused to visit me and won't even write.
He opens every letter I send to Sophie, takes out the cash and returns the letter unread via Dad. Sophie never seems to be about if I call round. I send as much as I can each month for her. Suspect she doesn't know anything about it.

Eventually the court case for access took place. Although Joanna was given access to Sophie, the latter said she did not want to see her mother again, so the girl's wishes were adhered to. Joanna's wishes were not considered.

When Sophie won a prize at school, Joanna was not informed and received an admonishment from the Priest, who told her that he had expected more from her. Joanna made an appointment to see him and informed him that she had not been told of the event. She also reported that the Deputy Head of Sophie's school had returned the letter that she had sent to her daughter 'on the instruction of her father, who has care and control and thought it would upset her too much to receive it.'

As Joanna did not hear from the Priest again, she presumed that Julian had won a little battle in the war he was waging. She did not care too much. She was happy with Hugh and despite the many problems, they knew that they would overcome them.

Julian continued to write demanding notes, usually concerning financial issues. Joanna paid for Sophie's trips and her accommodation at university. She insisted that she paid it directly into her daughter's bank account in the hope that she would realise that the money came from her. After all, Joanna continued to love her, even if they were unable to meet.

January 1987
Saw Sophie in the kitchen with her boyfriend when I visited Dad this
week. Dad says it is serious. I knocked on the door when I left, but no-one
opened it and they went into the lounge. Oh how it hurts . . .

Joanna's father was rushed to hospital in September. He had
been starving himself to death, had become so weak that he
had fallen as he had tried to get to the bathroom. He was
discovered by a neighbour who visited daily to ensure that he
was OK. She phoned the Service, who contacted Joanna in
the school where she was assessing a child.

There were many problems, including Julian trying
to convince the Hospital that he was the next of kin. It
resulted in a tremendous row in the ward between a
furious Joanna and the nurse who was on duty. Patrick
was consulted. He wanted to go to Leamington so that he
could be near his daughter and the niece who he nearly
adopted pre war.
Julian never forgave Joanna for thwarting his plans for her
father.

The most hurtful time came for Joanna when she met an old
friend in the supermarket who told her that Sophie was to be
married. No one had informed her—and the cheque that she
sent that night was never cashed.

Some years later, Hugh suggested that Joanna try to trace
Sophie through the Electoral Roll. Life without contact
with your child is pretty grim. Steven had occasionally
answered phone calls, but he had changed his surname to
that of Julian—so they were obviously closer than they used
to be. It worked. Joanna at least knew where her daughter
was.

However, when Joanna called on her, the door was
slammed in her face. Sophie was obviously pregnant and
Joanna eventually heard on the grape vine that she was
a grandmother to a little girl. Joan, Joanna's godmother,
unexpectedly wrote and gave her some details so that she
knew the child was named Maria and that she was dark, like
her father.

October 1994
Had a letter from Sheila today; she gets all the gossip at school. Don't know what I'll do when she retires at the end of the year. Sophie has had another baby. A boy.

March 1995
Saw Elaine in the supermarket—my new grandson's name is Louis or lewis, she wasn't sure. Wish I could see him. Perhaps in the future . . .

Chapter 21   By The Sea

For Joanna life with Hugh was in stark contrast to that with Julian. In her new relationship she was able to laugh with her partner. They shared the same sense of humour and found themselves laughing at each others jokes whilst others kept straight faces. They enjoyed play on words, the same sort of literature, appreciated all types of music (tapping out the rhythm of the rock songs or smiling contentedly at the beautiful ballads). They made positive comments about all events, encouraging each other in all aspects of life. They felt relaxed in their small flat, loving the physical contact with another being, cuddling cosily together on the sofa in front of the television or when listening to music. Hugh played his repertoire of songs on the guitar, choosing ones that contained lyrics of love. He occasionally wrote special songs for Joanna which she cherished. They chose cards for every anniversary and occasion, writing loving messages and poems at every opportunity. Their love of nature led to walks in the countryside, where they held onto each others hand for miles or exchanged private kisses in woods and meadows. How different from the joyless, sterile existence with jaundiced Julian.

Their life was filled with joy, some tears (usually connected to their daughters) and passionate love.

When they retired, after an unforgettable send-off from the school that had opened the door of true love for them, they decided to move to the seaside. They bought a house with wonderful views which looked out over the sea and old town.

They became interested in family history and began to delve into their pasts.

Hugh had no difficulty. He found that he came from landed gentry in Cornwall on one side and stone masons on the other.

Joanna, on the other hand, had the maiden name of her birth mother but no father's name on the birth certificate that she had been given in later years. She had given little thought to her birth parentage when Patrick and Pamela were alive, but now there was no one to hurt if she delved into unknown waters. There was a duplicated document from Church Welfare, which showed her birth mother's address in Sleaford, Lincolnshire but that she had been reluctant to divulge details of her father.

With these details, the Internet is an amazing tool and Joanna spent many hours scouring its pages. As she knew her maiden name she searched for the name 'Jackson'. The list was huge. She narrowed it down to the Lincolnshire area.

At last she was able to gain information about Amy Jackson (nee Rogers). She was amazed that her birth mother was born in1913, (only seven years after her adoptive Mum) which confirmed that she was not a young girl who had become pregnant by a young airman, but a more mature woman who had given birth to her. It would be interesting to see if she had traced the correct Amy Rogers. The only way to find out was to send away for the official documentation of her mother's birth, marriage and possible death in the form of certificates. She waited with bated breath.

It was a constant source of conversation when Joanna and Hugh took walks along the promenade. Until now, Joanna had rarely had a desire to know more of her origins, but finding names that matched her own held an excitement for her.

One morning the post thudded onto the mat. Hugh was always teasing his wife about her excitement over the arrival of mail, but she still ran down for it with enthusiasm!

The certificates had arrived and when Joanna opened them she found a few surprises.

The Birth Certificate showed that her mother was indeed born in 1913 and was older than Joanna had always imagined. Joanna had been born when her mother was 32 years old!

The marriage certificate showed that Amy, a domestic cook, was married to a turner in the RAF, William Jackson, in

1934. When she read the marriage certificate, it became obvious to Joanna that she was born to a married woman rather than a young innocent girl. Joanna had always understood from her adopted parents that she was the result of a liaison between her mother and an American airman, who was stationed at a nearby base. She had never considered that her mother might be a married woman!

The death certificate made her gasp. Despite being born in East Anglia, her mother had died in a Nursing Home, which was 500 yards from their own home. A Norma Jackson had registered the death. Her address was only three streets from her and Hugh's house. She was speechless. Hugh looked at her and Joanna passed the certificate across to him.

"Good Lord. If we had tried to make investigations earlier you would probably have met your mother."

"Yes. But don't you see? This woman is probably a sister-in-law. I'll have to investigate."

"O.K. Soon as I've checked the e-mails you can do a postcode check."

"Yes. And I'll look in the Electoral Rolls," she said.

During the search Joanna discovered that for some years there had been a George Jackson, as well as a Norma Jackson, at the address on the death certificate, but the last year only recorded Norma's name.

"We'll check it out at the Town Hall, when we go into town tomorrow," suggested Hugh.

Joanna could not sleep. In the morning they asked at the desk at the Town Hall if it was possible to discover who lived at known addresses. Joanna was questioned about the circumstances of her request. Because she was able to produce documents, she learned that George Jackson was deceased but that his wife still lived in the house.

The next step was to make contact with Norma Jackson.

Joanna decided that she would write to her and suggest that Norma might be her sister-in-law. She decided to give her the e-mail address but not the phone number as Joanna was not keen on telephones at the best of times, and this might prove stressful for all concerned.

She posted the letter on Friday so that everyone had a weekend to think things through. When nothing came in the post on Monday she was not over worried. When she returned from an extra duty at the local Hospice the next day, she felt a little disappointed to find there was still no reply. She took off her coat and noticed that the telephone message light was blinking. She pressed play, to hear a voice introducing herself as Norma Jackson and asking her to phone.

Joanna dialled the number.

"Hello. Norma Jackson speaking."

"Hello. It's Joanna here."

"Ah. Are you from a newspaper or anything like that?"

"NO." answered a bemused Joanna.

"Well you can't be too careful in this day and age. I'll ask you a few questions if you don't mind."

"O.K."

"Why do you think we might be related?"

Joanna explained about the certificates and how she had traced the person who had registered her birth mother's death. When she had finished, Norma asked,

"Where were you brought up?"

"Stamford in Lincolnshire."

"Um. Well I think I may be your sister, not your sister-in-law."

"Oh . . . I see."

"The best thing we could do is meet. When are you free?"

They discussed when would be convenient and found that the only time they were both free that week was that afternoon. Joanna was elated.

She had loved her parents dearly, but with the constant talk of finding ones roots, she was delighted to join the masses and discover her background. Who would have thought that she had a sister so near?
When Hugh arrived home for his lunch, Joanna informed him that she was off to meet her sister. He was more sceptical than his excited wife, but knew that she had to put her mind at rest—otherwise, she would be impossible to live with!

At 2o'clock, Joanna waited at the gate for the red car that her possible sister was driving. She pulled in and as Norma lent across to open the door, she looked Joanna up and down and said,

"Oh yes. You're my sister. You're the spitting image of my mother."

—0—

Parted in Lincolnshire at the time of war when aircraft filled the skies, their lives were re-joined at the seaside town of Weston-Super-Mare sixty-two years later.

Such a waste of sisterly time, it would be difficult to make the close contact enjoyed by most siblings. However, Joanna's pulse was racing and her heart was beating so fast that she could hardly breathe. She had never expected to feel so many emotions.

They made their way to the café on the seafront and Joanna learned that Norma did not share the love of the seaside town that already meant so much to her and Hugh. They talked about their offspring and their disappointments in life. There were some similarities in their ability to choose a husband, but Joanna knew that she had learned from her mistakes. Norma said that she felt unsure about her learning curve. They laughed and joked; probably to hide the roller coaster of emotion that they were experiencing. After two hours, they thought they should make their way back up the promenade.

Joanna had not meant to cry when they said their au revoirs. She just dissolved into tears when Norma had put her arms round her for a final hug. Fortunately, Joanna's new found half-sister told her that it was just the sort of reaction that their mother would have had, and she did not seem to mind.

That evening she shared her feelings with Hugh. The photographs that Norma and she had shown each other were uppermost in Joanna's mind. She could not believe that she looked so like her birth mother, though she had few regrets that she had not met her. Joanna knew that she had experienced a wonderful life and Norma's accounts of her childhood made her realise that she had been very lucky to have been adopted by the Hendersons. It had given her opportunities that her half-sister had not enjoyed. She was excited that she and Norma had made contact and that she knew more about her birth family.

They had decided to refer to Amy as 'our mother' so that Joanna could still use 'my mother' in relation to Pamela Henderson, who had meant so much to her. Joanna knew that her adopted family would always be part of her life. Her cousins (the only generation alive) were all loved and cherished by her. She knew them and how they fitted into the lives of her 'parents' and they would not be deserted for this new family.

As Joanna reflected on the meeting with her new-found sister, she wondered if they would have anything in common. How much was life linked into inherited genes, and how much was it influenced by their very different home-lives? Would the old 'nature/nurture' debate roll on? What would finding a sister when they were both in their sixties mean to both of these 'war babies', who were now drawing their pensions? Only time would tell.

Perhaps finding this family would bring further joy. Perhaps one day there will be another story to tell.

Lightning Source UK Ltd.
Milton Keynes UK
UKOW050856260112

186071UK00001B/28/P